REAL LIFE FAITH

Bible Companions for Catholic Teens

Mary Elizabeth Sperry

Liguori
LIGUORI, MISSOURI

Imprimi Potest:
Harry Grile, CSsR, Provincial
Denver Province, The Redemptorists

Published by Liguori Publications
Liguori, Missouri 63057

To order, call 800-325-9521
www.liguori.org

Library of Congress Cataloging-in-Publication Data

Sperry, Mary Elizabeth.
 Real life faith : Bible companions for Catholic teens / Mary Elizabeth Sperry.
 —First Edition.
    pages cm
 1. Catholic teenagers—Religious life. 2. Catholic teenagers—Conduct of life.
 3. Bible—Biography. I. Title.
 BX2355.S64 2014
 248.8'3—dc23
                                        2014001722
 p ISBN: 978-0-7648-2396-1
 e ISBN: 978-0-7648-6887-0

Liguori Publications, a nonprofit corporation, is an apostolate of The Redemptorists. To learn more about The Redemptorists, visit Redemptorists.com.

Printed in the United States of America
18 17 16 15 14 / 5 4 3 2 1
First Edition

Contents

Dedication

For the Bensch and Vance families, especially Jan.

You are the best. Thank you for everything.

Acknowledgments

This book was written in the midst of a very difficult year. So many people I love, family and friends, have suffered so much fear and pain and loss. Only my faith (especially the joy, hope, and compassion evidenced so fully by Pope Francis) and the kindness of many people in my life have pulled me through this valley of shadows. It's time to say thank you to:

My supervisors, Paul Henderson and Helen Osman, who have supported my writing from the beginning.

Luis Media, Christy Hicks, and Julia DiSalvo, who offered great advice and support during the writing process.

My friends, who kept insisting that I could finish writing, even when I doubted it: Noreen, Vicki, Jennifer, Lisa, Stephen, Lisa, Rae Ann, and Deb.

Henry, my godson. You have no idea how much your presence here has blessed my life.

Chris, my biggest cheerleader and my greatest support. I couldn't have done it without you. You don't realize how amazing you are.

Hershey, my daily reminder of what unconditional love looks like.

Finally, to my family: my mother, Kay, who amazes me with her capacity to love; my sisters, Kathy and Carol Ann; and my beloved father, who left us just before I started this book. I love you. Thank you.

Introduction

[W]e are surrounded by so great a cloud of witnesses....

HEBREWS 12:1

Parts of the Bible are more than 4,000 years old. The people who wrote it lived thousands of miles away from us. Their lives focused around fishing and harvest and trades learned from their parents. How in the world could the Bible have anything to say to us? What can the people in the Bible teach us? After all, they lived in such a different world!

You might be surprised! Though parts of their lives were very different, the people in the Bible faced many of the same challenges we face today: peer pressure, feeling left out, feeling like no one took them seriously, looking for real friends, seeking good advice, and so on. Sound familiar?

When people of the Bible faced great challenges, they turned to God for the help they needed. In each chapter of this book, we'll look at one person from the Bible and how his or her story can help us see our lives in a new light. We'll look at what the Bible teaches us about the person's life and what that person can teach us. Each of these Bible companions illustrates a special quality that helps us grow closer to God and become the people we want to be—and the people God wants us to be. Each chapter includes questions to help you think about what you've read and maybe discuss it with your friends or youth group. Plus there are suggested Bible passages if you'd like to read more about the person.

You don't need to read this book straight through like a novel or a textbook. Feel free to skip around and read about the people who interest you the most—or about the ones who model qualities you'd like to acquire.

Even though these Bible companions walked the earth thousands of years ago, they wait to walk with you, helping you to find the path that will lead you to God.

Chapter 1

Cassidy: A Real-Life Abel

The Lord looked with favor on Abel and his offering.

Genesis 4:4

Cassidy loved running cross-country. She wasn't the team star or anything like that. In fact, she'd never medaled in any competition. But even though she wasn't the fastest runner, she always tried her hardest. She showed up at every practice and paid attention to the drills rather than chatting with her teammates. Every day, Cassidy stretched, and she did strength training a few times a week. She watched what she ate—even limiting how often she ate potato chips, her favorite snack. Instead of texting friends and chatting online, she made sure she got enough sleep every night so she'd be at her best for cross-country practice after school.

Now, Cassidy wasn't one-dimensional. Cross-country wasn't her whole life. She was a good (but not great) student. She was a member of a few clubs and an active participant in her church's youth ministry. She wasn't a standout in anything she did, but she made a promise to herself that whatever she decided to do, she'd give it her very best. Sometimes she wondered if it was worth it. Why bother to work so hard if no one else did? Why give her best if she would never *be* the best?

Who Is Abel?

The Bible doesn't tell us much about Abel. In fact, it never records a single word he spoke. We know Abel was the second son of Adam and Eve. He had an older brother named Cain. When they grew up, Cain became a farmer, and Abel was a herder—probably of sheep and goats.

Both Cain and Abel offered sacrifices to God, offering up some of what they produced to the Lord. Cain offered some of the crops he had grown, and Abel offered the first animals born into his flock. God accepted Abel's offering, but he did not accept the sacrifice offered by Cain. The Book of Genesis doesn't tell us why God didn't accept Cain's offering. However, the Letter to the Hebrews suggests that Abel made his sacrifice to God in faith. Because of Abel's faith, his sacrifice was acceptable. This explanation suggests that Cain's motives in offering sacrifice may not have been as pure, but we can't tell from what is recorded in Genesis.

We do know that Cain was very upset when God rejected his sacrifice, and he became very jealous of Abel—so jealous, in fact, that Cain asked Abel to go with him into the fields. When they got to the field, Cain attacked and killed his brother, leaving his body in the field. Thus, Abel was the first murder victim.

While Abel's story ends there, Cain's does not. God, who knows what Cain has done, asks him where Abel is. Cain claims not to know and asks, "Am I my brother's keeper?" (Genesis 4:9). God charges Cain with the murder of his brother and exiles Cain from the land that he has shared with his family, condemning him to wander the earth. But despite his grievous sin, God does not harm Cain physically. In fact, God offers him protection so that no one will harm him.

What Can Abel Teach Us?

For a guy who doesn't have even one recorded line in the whole Bible, Abel can teach us a lot. He teaches us about the importance of integrity and of giving God our best.

From the little we know of him, Abel was a man of integrity, acting from his faith to make a true sacrifice to the God he worshiped. Integrity is one of those words people use without thinking about what it means. Integrity comes from a root word meaning "whole." It means that the whole you—all the elements of your life—agree with one another. You aren't two-faced, the sort of person who behaves one way around one group of friends and a completely different way around another group. The way you behave is consistent with what you claim to believe. When you say you value something, you show it through your actions. So, for example, if you claim to value honesty, you don't tell lies or exaggerate the truth. Being a person of integrity means that people can rely on your word, knowing that you will back it up by what you do.

Integrity is an important part of being a holy person. It's not by accident that "whole" and "holy" sound so much alike. Being holy means your faith must infuse your whole life—not just for an hour at church each Sunday. You can't claim to be a person who follows Jesus unless you are willing to take steps to grow in your relationship with him. Since you can't be in a relationship with someone you don't know, you will want to learn more about your faith, even after you no longer have formal religious-education classes. Your faith will inform all aspects of your life, from who your friends are to how you spend your free time to what career you will pursue.

Deciding what you will do with your life is one of the biggest decisions facing most young people. Your parents, friends, counselors, and others may offer advice, helping you identify your skills and interests and find career choices that use those skills and appeal to those interests. As a person of faith, however, your first question should be, "What is God calling me to do?" God calls each person to place his or her gifts at the service of the community and the kingdom of God.

Discerning God's will for you is something you will do throughout your life. However, in the years immediately ahead of you, discerning your vocation will be an important task. A vocation is more than a career choice. It is the way God calls you to live in the world to serve the kingdom. You may be called to marriage and family life. You may be called to live as a single person. You may even be called to dedicate your life to the service of God's people in the priesthood or consecrated life. Prayer, regular reception of the Eucharist and celebration of the sacrament of penance, and the advice of reliable counselors and quiet listening will help you to learn God's will for you. Seeking and following God's path will lead you to the greatest peace and fulfillment.

Whatever path you choose, follow Abel's example. Abel chose to be a shepherd, and he offered the very best of his flock as a sacrifice to God. In the same way, we should offer God our very best in everything we do. Even if the tasks we face are not specifically religious (like attending Mass or helping on a service project), we can still offer our efforts to God. Whether it is schoolwork, chores, extracurricular activities, or helping a friend, we can give God our very best, asking that he accept all we do and have and are. The first step in offering ourselves to God is recognizing that, on our own, we can do nothing. Everything we do and have and are is a gift from God. Like Abel, by giving our best and caring for our brothers and sisters, we offer these gifts back to God in gratitude.

Sacrifice

When we hear the word "sacrifice," we think about giving something up. For example, our Lenten sacrifice might be to give up a favorite snack food or a video game. But sacrifice is much more than that. The English word "sacrifice" actually comes from two Latin words that mean "to make holy." So sacrifice isn't just about giving something up. It is about offering something to God to make it holy. The goal of our sacrifice should be to grow in holiness.

Sacrifice begins by understanding that everything we have is a gift from God. By offering our gifts back to God, we show our gratitude and give God the praise and honor he deserves. We ask God to receive us and make us holy. We strive to use our gifts to serve God and others. Like Abel, we offer God the best we have, just because he's God.

The most perfect sacrifice we can offer is the sacrifice of the Mass, the holy Eucharist. In the Mass, we remember, celebrate, and re-present the sacrifice of Jesus on the cross, the sacrifice that is our salvation. In the Mass, we gather our words and actions, our hopes and fears, our joys and sorrows, and join them to Jesus' sacrifice, offering them to the Father in the Holy Spirit. We ask the Father to accept our sacrifice as he accepted the sacrifice of his servant Abel. And we receive Holy Communion, the Body of Christ, asking Jesus to live in us so that we may be made holy, as he is holy.

Farmers and Herders

Cain and Abel are the first examples of two of the most common occupations in the Bible: farmers and herders. People need to eat, so it isn't surprising that the first jobs that appear focus on making sure that people have food. For the most part, farmers tend to settle and work in one place. They live where there's good soil and access to water for a long period of time—at least long enough to plant and harvest a crop. They need to store food from one harvest to the next. Herders, on the other hand, are typically nomadic. They move from place to place, living in tents, looking for pasture and water for their flocks. Depending on the availability of food and water, they may range over a small or a large territory. They roam farther when food and water are hard to find.

Read More About Abel

> Genesis 4:1–16
> Hebrews 11:4

Questions to Think About

1. How do I give back to God the gifts he has given me?

2. What keeps me from giving God my best?

3. Do I celebrate others' gifts, or am I jealous of them?

Prayer

> *Heavenly Father,*
> *thank you for the many gifts you have given me*
> *that help me in life.*
> *Help me to always use them*
> *to serve you and your people,*
> *so that I may praise you in all that I do.*
> *Amen.*

Chapter 2

Taylor: A Real-Life Joseph

But Joseph replied to them: "Do not fear. Can I take the place of God? Even though you meant harm to me, God meant it for good."

Genesis 50:19–20

Taylor wasn't the most popular girl in school, but she had a great group of friends. She really loved sitting with them at lunch, studying together, and hanging out on weekends. Like any high school student, she had good days and bad days. But generally things were pretty good—until they weren't.

At first, it was kind of subtle. People looked at Taylor oddly when she walked down the hall, or they'd suddenly stop talking when she entered a room. Then she started to see hints on social media: people unfriending her or mentioning parties she wasn't invited to attend. Finally, she got to the source. A nasty rumor about her had spread throughout the school, making people question whether she was reliable or even the sort of person she seemed to be. Even though the rumor shocked her, the biggest shock was yet to come. She learned that the source of the rumor was Julie, her friend!

Taylor confronted Julie, asking why she had spread such lies. Crying, Julie explained that she was tired of her parents comparing her negatively to Taylor, always asking why Julie couldn't be more like Taylor. Finally stressed to her breaking point, Julie blurted out the first lie that came to mind. From there, the story raged out of control, spreading among parents, students, and teachers. Julie said over and over how sorry she was and asked Taylor to forgive her. Taylor did forgive Julie, and together they worked to make sure that people knew the rumors were lies.

Who Is Joseph?

Joseph was one of the sons of Jacob (also known as Israel). Jacob had twelve sons by four different women: Leah and Rachel, who were sisters, and their servants, Bilhah and Zilpah. Rachel was Jacob's favorite wife, the love of his life. He favored the two sons she bore: Joseph and Benjamin. Joseph was Jacob's favorite son by far. Jacob even gave Joseph expensive gifts. Not surprisingly, Joseph wasn't very popular with his brothers. They gave him the cold shoulder, refusing to talk to him. To tell the truth, even without the special privileges, Joseph wasn't an easy guy to like. He worked with his brothers, watching the flocks in the fields, but he also acted as his father's informant, carrying bad reports about his brothers. In other words, he was a tattletale. Joseph also had a special gift from God. He was a dreamer and an interpreter of dreams.

Once, Joseph shared a dream he had that his brothers would end up serving him. After that prediction, his brothers had had enough. When Joseph came to meet them in the fields, they grabbed him and imprisoned him in a cistern. While the original plan was to kill Joseph and blame his death on wild animals, cooler heads prevailed, and his brothers sold him to some travelers who, in turn, sold Joseph as a slave in Egypt.

Joseph's time in Egypt began pretty well. He was purchased by a powerful man who made Joseph his personal attendant. Joseph was still a slave, but he was treated well. But rocky waters were ahead. His master's wife became infatuated with Joseph and tried to seduce him. When Joseph refused her advances, she accused him of assaulting her. His master, believing that Joseph had betrayed his trust, had Joseph thrown in prison.

Even in prison, Joseph made the best of his lot with the help of the Lord. The jailer trusted him and gave Joseph special privileges. While in jail, two of Joseph's fellow prisoners had dreams that troubled them. Joseph used his gift of interpretation to help them understand the meaning of their dreams, giving one very good news and the other very bad news. The man who got the good news was restored to his former position in service to Pharaoh, the ruler of Egypt.

When Pharaoh had dreams that troubled him, this servant remembered Joseph and had him released from prison to interpret Pharaoh's dreams. Joseph said Pharaoh's dreams were a warning that, after seven years of abundant harvests, Egypt would suffer seven years of devastating famine. To preserve the nation during the famine, Joseph recommended appointing someone to oversee the storage of the extra food produced during the years of abundance. This food could be rationed to the people during the years of famine so they wouldn't starve. Pharaoh was so pleased with the idea that he put Joseph in charge of the project.

Things happened just as Joseph had predicted. As the famine deepened, having access to the food that Joseph had stored increased Pharaoh's wealth and power. As Pharaoh grew more powerful, so did Joseph. That power did not stop at Egypt's borders. Because the famine spread throughout the whole region, people from other countries came to Egypt to get the rations they needed to survive.

In time, the famine hit the land of Canaan, where Jacob lived with his remaining sons. When they ran out of food, the sons decided to go to Egypt to get the food they needed. Of course, they had no idea that the second-most powerful man in Egypt was the brother they'd sold into slavery years before! Leaving Joseph's full brother Benjamin at home to take care of Jacob, the other brothers traveled to Egypt to buy food. Seeing them come to get rations, Joseph recognized his brothers. He accused them of being spies who had come to assess Egypt's weaknesses during the famine. Ultimately, he agreed to allow them to go home, though he kept one brother as a prisoner. However, he told the other brothers that they couldn't come back for more food without bringing the youngest brother to prove their story. Joseph had his servants give his brothers food and even return the money they had brought to pay for the rations.

When Jacob and his sons had eaten all of the food they'd brought from Egypt, they had to go back for more. Remembering Joseph's demand, they took the youngest, Benjamin, with them, to Jacob's great dismay. Upon their arrival in Egypt, Joseph greeted them. The brothers offered to return the money that Joseph had given back after their initial purchase of food. After spending some time with them, Joseph sent them home with plenty of food, plus the money they'd brought, but not before telling one of his servants to hide a silver goblet in Benjamin's bag. After his brothers left, Joseph sent his steward to overtake them, accusing them of stealing the goblet. The brothers returned to Egypt once again, and Joseph said the brother who had stolen the goblet would become his slave, but the rest could go. Of course, the cup was in Benjamin's bag. Judah offered to stay in Egypt in Benjamin's place, fearing Jacob would die in grief over the loss of a second son by Rachel.

Recognizing that his brothers had learned their lesson, Joseph revealed his identity to his brothers and offered them his forgiveness, noting that God had brought good from their evil act. He invited his brothers to return to Canaan to bring their families and Jacob to Egypt where they could live in peace and prosperity, protected by the power of the brother they had once betrayed.

What Can Joseph Teach Us?

Being in charge of the only food available in the region is a source of great power, but the gift of forgiveness has a power all its own. Joseph certainly knew that power, and he used it well. He can teach us how to be people of forgiveness and reconciliation.

For Joseph and for us, the gift of forgiveness is rooted in our relationship with God. Because Joseph knew that the Lord was with him, he was able to make the best of any situation in which he found himself. He didn't let bitterness or the bad breaks he faced harden his heart to the people around him. Bitterness, cynicism, and self-pity crowd out forgiveness. Trust in the Lord and the sure knowledge that you matter to God provide fertile ground for forgiveness to grow.

Another important aspect of becoming a more forgiving person is to have a healthy and realistic self-image. Knowing our own faults makes it easier to recognize and forgive the faults of others. In the same way, if we have experienced the gift of God's forgiveness in the sacrament of penance, we may be willing to share the gift of forgiveness with people who have hurt us.

Forgiving someone can be very difficult, particularly if the injury was great. It can mean opening yourself to the risk of even more pain. Forgiving someone doesn't mean that you have to restore the person to a place of trust immediately—or ever. Joseph tested his brothers to make sure they had learned their lesson before he reestablished his relationship with them. Giving someone a chance to prove he has changed can be frightening. The person you forgave could hurt you again or take you for granted. Still, all power comes with risk. Taking the risk to forgive opens your heart even more to the hope of peace and reconciliation and to the receiving and sharing of God's love.

Drought and Famine

The people we meet in the Bible lived close to the land. Their survival depended on food grown, caught, raised, or hunted nearby and on access to reliable sources of water. A drought was devastating on two levels. It dried up wells, meaning less water for drinking and cooking. Plus, less water was available for livestock and crops. Without grass to eat, sheep and goats would die. Without rain or water for irrigation, crops would fail. Even a relatively short drought could cause widespread hunger. A longer drought could cause famine, and entire populations would face the real possibility of starvation. The famine about which Joseph warned Pharaoh lasted seven years. Without Joseph's advance planning, the effects would have been catastrophic.

Unfortunately, drought and famine didn't end in biblical times. Even today, much of the world's population lacks access to clean drinking water. In many countries, women and girls walk miles each day, carrying heavy containers to and from the well or other water source. All too often, the water is not clean, fostering the spread of disease. The time needed to get water prevents many girls from going to school.

Deforestation and the erosion of topsoil have ravaged farmland and led to famine in many places. Hunger and disease prey on the weak, especially the very old and the very young. Even in the United States, all too many people lack secure access to food, meaning they are not sure if they will have sufficient food to last the week—or even the day. In our world of seeming abundance, many people must do without the basic necessities of life. Like Joseph, may we seek out ways to provide for their needs.

Egypt in the Bible

When we think of Egypt, we probably think of pyramids and mummies, but Egypt plays a very interesting symbolic role in the Bible. For the most part, Egypt is defined by what it is not. It is not the Promised Land where the children of Israel live in freedom as God's Chosen People. Rather, Egypt is a place of slavery, a place where the Israelites are distanced from their heritage. Throughout the Bible, the people of Israel remember that God brought them out of Egypt and into the "land flowing with milk and honey" (Exodus 3:8), the Promised Land. They recall that God led them from slavery and into freedom.

The Gospel of Matthew (chapter 2) tells us that Joseph (the other Joseph, Jesus' foster father) took Mary and Jesus to Egypt to protect Jesus from Herod. King Herod saw Jesus as a threat to his power and wanted to kill him. Only after Herod's death could the Holy Family return to the land of Israel. Ultimately, through his cross, Jesus would offer us salvation, leading us from slavery to sin to a life of freedom as the children of God.

Read More About Joseph

Genesis 37, 39—48, 50

Questions to Think About

1. Has anyone ever done something that truly hurt you? How did you respond?

2. What obstacles keep you from offering forgiveness?

3. What benefits does offering forgiveness bring?

Prayer

Jesus,
sometimes when I'm hurt,
it's hard to forgive those who have hurt me.
Help me to be more like you in bringing
forgiveness and reconciliation to those who need it most.
Amen.

Chapter 3

Beatriz: A Real-Life Miriam

Then the prophet Miriam, Aaron's sister, took a tambourine in her hand, while all the women went out after her with tambourines, dancing; and she responded to them:

Sing to the LORD, for he is gloriously triumphant; horse and chariot he has cast into the sea.

EXODUS 15:20–21

Beatriz was a good kid. Everyone said so—when they bothered to notice her. It wasn't intentional. She just wasn't the kind of person you notice. She didn't dress in crazy clothes or dye her hair green. She went to class, got OK grades, volunteered with the youth-ministry group, and worked at a clothing store in the mall. The real star was her younger brother, Carlos. Even though he was a sophomore and she was a senior, he was the one everyone knew. He was the goalie for the district champion soccer team and a leader on the student council. He was even elected Snow King at the winter formal. Beatriz helped with the decorations. Beatriz loved Carlos. He was a great little brother. But sometimes, it would be nice if someone asked about her first. She was beginning to think her first name was "Where's Carlos?" Didn't she matter?

Who Is Miriam?

Like Beatriz, Miriam was a big sister—Moses' and Aaron's big sister. She got less attention because she wasn't a great speaker like Aaron, and she didn't convey God's words and wonders like Moses did, leading the Hebrew people from slavery to freedom. But even though she may not have been as well-known as her brothers, she played an important role in the story of her people.

In fact, without Miriam, Moses might never have gotten his chance to lead the people. Before Moses was born, the Hebrew people lived as slaves in the land of Egypt. Concerned about the growing number of Hebrew people in the country, Pharaoh (the ruler of Egypt) declared that all boy children born to Hebrew women should be drowned in the Nile River at birth. Not wanting to lose her son, Moses' mother placed him in a basket that she hid in the reeds along the Nile, setting Miriam to keep watch. Miriam watched over her baby brother until Pharaoh's daughter saw him while walking along the shore. Once Pharaoh's daughter took charge of Moses, Miriam came forward and offered her mother to care for the child, assuring that he would be raised with care and love.

The Book of Exodus later tells that God worked powerful signs to free the Hebrew people from slavery, subjecting the Egyptians to ten plagues, culminating in the death of each firstborn son among the Egyptians. Finally set free by Pharaoh, the Israelites began their journey to the Promised Land. God continued to protect them on the way. Caught between the Egyptian army and the Red Sea, God parted the waters of the sea so the Israelites could pass through safely. When the Egyptian army followed them into the sea, God allowed the waters to flow back, destroying the entire army. In relief and thanksgiving, Miriam picked up her tambourine and led the women in a song of praise to the Lord who had set them free and kept them safe.

The next time we see Miriam is far less flattering. In the midst of the Israelites' forty years of wandering in the desert from Egypt to the Promised Land, Miriam and Aaron become jealous of Moses' authority in the community and of his close relationship with God. After all, only Moses speaks with God face to face. On the pretext of pointing out the inappropriateness of Moses' marriage to a non-Hebrew woman, Miriam and Aaron begin to criticize Moses and promote their own roles as leaders in the community. Moses was too humble to fight his brother and sister, but God called them to account. Calling Aaron and Miriam into his presence, God made it very clear that Moses was his chosen prophet and that Miriam and Aaron should not interfere with God's plan. As punishment for their jealousy and disobedience, God struck Miriam with a skin disease that forced her to live apart from the community. Out of respect for her, the Israelites did not abandon her in the desert. Instead, they waited a week for her illness to be healed. Only when she was well enough to rejoin the community did the people continue their journey. Eventually, the Bible notes, she died and was buried in the desert. Like her brothers, Miriam never set foot in the Promised Land.

What Can Miriam Teach Us?

Even though she lived almost 6,000 years ago, Miriam can help us live a holy life today. She models three virtues everyone should strive to cultivate: perseverance, responsibility, and willingness to praise God.

Miriam persevered. She was really good at waiting, which was a good thing since she did a lot of it! She spent time waiting on the banks of the Nile, watching over her baby brother, keeping him safe and hoping that someone would come along to care for him. Can you imagine how slowly each minute seemed to pass as she watched and waited? How afraid and alone she must have felt, with no one to rely on except for God. How worried she must have been for her baby brother—and for her mother, who was breaking the law by trying to save her son.

Miriam also waited during the seven days when she had to live outside the camp, her skin disfigured by disease. She was probably itchy and uncomfortable from the illness, but she must have felt guilty, too. Her relationship with her brother, Moses, and his wife had been damaged by her charges against his wife and by her attempt to diminish Moses' position. It seems likely that her relationship with Aaron had been damaged, since she bore the punishment for what they both did. Feeling guilty can make you distant, even from those you love. Even though she was respected by the community, she had to feel bad about making them wait for her, making a long journey even longer. But most of all, she had damaged her relationship with God, questioning his decision to make Moses his prophet, after all God had done for the people of Israel: freeing them from slavery in Egypt, parting the Red Sea so they could pass through safely, giving them food and water in the desert, and inviting the people of Israel to be his own special people. When you feel guilty and distant from those you love, time passes even more slowly, making perseverance even harder.

Finally, Miriam waited—and persevered—during the Israelites' forty-year journey through the desert. It was a long and difficult journey. The Israelites were surrounded by enemies as well as the dangers of the desert. Though God provided food and water, the food was limited to manna and quail—a far cry from the rich and varied diet the people had eaten during their time in Egypt. The people must have been frightened, bored, and disappointed—not the best traveling companions. And there was nowhere to go, no one new to meet. No one was exactly sure where they were going, when they would get there, or what they would find when they arrived. As a leader of the community, Miriam would have heard all of the complaints and felt responsible for helping the people stay the course.

Through all these trials, Miriam persevered, trusting that God would act: saving her brother, bringing her healing, leading the people to safety. Her faith allowed her to carry on, even when things seemed the darkest. She kept trusting, hoping, and believing. Even though she never saw the Promised Land and the fulfillment of her dreams, her people did. Ultimately, her perseverance paid off.

It's hard to wait for God in a world where everything is instant and on our schedule. Waiting two minutes for the microwave to nuke your popcorn can seem like forever. We watch our favorite TV shows on our schedule and customize our music playlists so we can hear the songs we want when we want. It's uncomfortable to let go of our agenda and wait for God's plans to work out. That's when we need to walk with Miriam, letting her show us how to wait for God to make his plan known.

Miriam can teach us responsibility as well. Though still a child herself, she took responsibility for watching over her baby brother, keeping him safe. During the journey through the desert, she shared responsibility for the community, serving as a leader among the women, helping them to keep moving toward the goal while taking care of the needs of everyday life. She also took responsibility for her mistakes. Though she was punished for her actions against Moses and his wife, the Bible never reports her complaining or whining or making excuses. She accepted her punishment and moved on. Because she took responsibility, the people gave her their respect, looking to her for advice and leadership. When she was stricken with a skin disease, the people waited for her to get better rather than moving on without her.

It's strange, isn't it? All too often we try to hide our mistakes or make excuses for them or even blame someone else, all because we don't want people to think less of us or to tease us about our failings. We are afraid that taking responsibility for our mistakes will make us look bad in others' eyes. In fact, the opposite is true. When we take responsibility for both the good and the bad that we do, people respect us more, not less. We become people they can count on, even when things are difficult.

The flip side of taking responsibility is giving credit where credit is due. When God led the Israelites through the Red Sea in safety, Miriam led the women in a song of praise and thanksgiving to God. She knew that Moses hadn't parted the sea with his own power, so she gave credit to God. And she wasn't afraid to show her love for God in public. This song and dance of praise was for all to see and hear.

It's tempting to take credit for the good things that happen to us and to think we've earned them through our own efforts. But it's important to remember that all good things come from God. We owe God our thanks and praise, and we have to be willing to share our love for God with those around us. We should never be afraid to thank God for the good things we have and to stand up for what we believe. Whenever we are impatient or embarrassed or afraid, we can be like Miriam!

The Israelites in Ancient Egypt

By the time of Miriam's birth, the Israelites had lived in Egypt for many generations. They had come to Egypt when Jacob's son, Joseph, was one of Pharaoh's top officials. Over the years, the Israelites had grown in power and influence—so much that they became a threat to the Egyptians. So the Egyptians forced the Israelites into slavery.

This slavery was not like the slavery that existed in the United States before the Civil War. The Israelites were not owned by individual Egyptians, and they could not be bought and sold. However, they had no rights and were forced to work on Egyptian building projects, making bricks. While they had food and shelter, they could not choose their work or leave Egypt. Their right to worship God was based on Pharaoh's whim.

Life in the Desert

Just because God liberated the Israelites from slavery in Egypt doesn't mean that all their problems were solved. Even though they had received gifts of clothes, jewelry, and money before they left Egypt, their lives were still very difficult. After all, there were no shopping malls in the desert where they could stop and pick up the things they needed.

In fact, the desert was full of dangers. The Israelites knew they were headed to the Promised Land, but they weren't sure exactly where it was, how long it would take to get there, or what they would find when they arrived. Even worse, their path was blocked by hostile nations willing to fight rather than let the Israelites go through. The land itself was dangerous, filled with snakes and scorpions whose bites could kill. Food was scarce and limited, especially compared to the bounty they had in Egypt. Imagine eating the same thing every day for forty years!

Read More About Miriam

Exodus 2
Exodus 15:20–21
Numbers 12
Numbers 20:1

Questions to Think About

1. What makes it hard to keep faith in God?
2. What makes my faith in him stronger?
3. How can I share my love for God with those around me?
4. How can I be more like Miriam?

Prayer

God our Father,
Miriam relied on you,
and you never let her down.
Help me to follow her example
and persevere in faith.
Help me bear my responsibilities,
knowing that you are always with me.
Like Miriam, may I never stop singing your praise! Amen.

Chapter 4

Lien: A Real-Life Joshua

Now Joshua, son of Nun, was filled with the spirit of wisdom,
since Moses had laid his hands upon him.

Deuteronomy 34:9

L ien was excited, but scared. She'd been invited to join the
student mentoring program. She'd be paired with a business
leader from the community for two years. During that time, Lien
and her mentor would meet regularly, discuss books and articles
they had both read, and work together to plan and execute at
least two community-service projects. By the time the two years
ended, Lien would be leading a project on her own, with advice
and support as needed from her mentor. The goal was to build
a new community of leaders who would pay the opportunity
forward when their time came.

Lien's parents had instilled in her the importance of giving
back to the community. As children, they had come to the United
States as refugees with little more than the clothes on their backs.
The local church had helped them find a place to live and set up a
household. Her parents were enrolled in the Catholic school and
started learning English. Now they had their own business. Her
mom was the president of the parish council and her dad was the
most ardent member of the Justice and Life Committee. Giving
back and leadership seemed to be in the family genes.

That's why Lien was nervous. Could she live up to her parents' and teachers' expectations? She knew she was a hard worker, but did she have what it takes to lead? What if she failed? What if no one followed her?

Who Is Joshua?

Joshua was one of the leaders of the Israelites as they traveled from Egypt to the Promised Land. He seems to have been one of the men who led the Israelites in battle, defending the people in the skirmishes they faced as they wandered in the desert. Later, Joshua was the only person allowed to accompany Moses when he met with God on Mount Sinai. (Joshua didn't actually converse with God the way Moses did. He waited for Moses at the foot of the mountain.) Joshua learned about being a leader from watching Moses.

Sometimes, Joshua was a slow learner. Leading the entire nation of Israel was a big responsibility, and Moses needed help. God told him to choose seventy elders respected by the people and to have them gather together. The Lord would anoint them with the Spirit so they could help Moses with the day-to-day governing of the people. Moses did as the Lord had requested, but two of the chosen elders did not make it to the gathering. Still, God gave them the gift of the Spirit. Joshua reacted angrily, wanting Moses to stop these men from exercising the power the Lord had given them. Even after years of watching Moses, Joshua still thought that leadership was about power and control.

While Joshua might not have been completely ready to lead yet, he understood the importance of standing up for his principles and beliefs. When Moses sent twelve scouts to look over the land of Canaan in preparation for the Israelites' entrance into the land, eleven of them came back recommending that the Israelites abandon their plan to go into the Promised Land. They had seen the might of the people living there, and they were afraid. Only Caleb counseled them to trust in the Lord's promise, believing that the Lord would not desert the Israelites in the face of their enemies. Despite the unpopularity of his position, Joshua stood with Caleb, announcing to the whole people that he trusted the Lord's promise.

Joshua would need to rely on his trust in God even more in the years ahead. Moses died before the Israelites entered the Promised Land. As Moses' trusted aide, mentored by Moses for years, Joshua was ready to take up the mantle of leadership. When Joshua became the leader of the Israelites, the Lord promised to be with him always, offering guidance and support.

With Joshua in the lead, the people got ready to cross the Jordan River and enter the Promised Land. When the priests carrying the Ark of the Covenant (which held the tablets on which God had written the Ten Commandments) stepped into the Jordan River, the water stopped flowing so that the people could cross on dry land. Joshua always remembered that God was the true leader of Israel, so he praised God for his goodness and called on the Israelite people to remember their covenant with the Lord by obeying his laws and keeping the religious festivals that the Lord had ordained.

Unfortunately for the Israelites, crossing the Jordan River was the easy part. Now that they were in the Promised Land, the Israelites needed territory where they could establish homes and farms. The next years were times of near-constant warfare as the Israelites captured the land they needed.

Their campaign began with Joshua's most famous battle: the Battle of Jericho. Jericho was a fortress city, surrounded by a thick wall, prepared to withstand a long siege. The Book of Joshua tells us that the Israelites went to Jericho for six days and marched around the city once each day. On the seventh day, they marched around the city seven times. On the seventh time, the priests leading the march blew on horns, and all the people answered with a tremendous shout. As the great spiritual says, they shouted so loudly that "the walls came tumbling down."

The Battle of Jericho is just the first of many battles that the people of Israel fought in their conquest of the land of Canaan. But even this string of successful battles did not complete Joshua's work. After the conquest came the even more difficult work of building a nation from a collection of often fractious tribes. But the people of Israel had one thing going for them—their relationship with the Lord.

In his final act as the leader of the Israelites, just before his death, Joshua reminded the people of this relationship. He gathered the people together and reminded them of all that the Lord had done for them: liberating them from slavery in Egypt, keeping them safe for forty years in the desert, giving them the Law to keep them on the right path, and giving them possession of the Promised Land.

Joshua reminded the people that the relationship was not one-sided. The people had to respond to God's invitation to be his people by obeying the Law he had given them. If they chose not to follow God's laws, the people were free to worship the gods of the neighboring peoples. Joshua stated clearly that his allegiance, and that of his household, would remain with the Lord who had done so much for them. For one final time, the people of Israel followed Joshua's lead, embracing once again their covenant with the Lord.

What Can Joshua Teach Us?

It would be too simple to say that Joshua can teach us how to lead. What does leadership mean? How should we exercise the responsibilities of leadership? Is there anything special about Christian leadership?

Very few people are born leaders, knowing how to lead effectively just by nature. Most good leaders are made, not born. Like Joshua, they learn how to lead by having a mentor who helps them develop the skills they need. One of the first things a leader needs to learn is that leadership isn't the same thing as power or control. A good leader doesn't force people to do what she wants them to do; she calls forth their best efforts for the good of the group, thinking about them before she thinks of herself. A good leader places herself at the service of the people.

A good leader needs to be willing to stand up for his principles, even when that's not a popular position. Always making the easy choice and going along with the crowd may seem like the right plan at first, but a good leader owes the people he leads his best judgment and his best effort to achieve the common good. A Christian leader needs to go one step further. A good Christian leader starts by being a good follower—of Jesus. A Christian leader strives, above all, by word and by deed, to lead people to Jesus.

The Conquest of Canaan

When the Israelites moved into the Promised Land, it was not unoccupied territory. There were people—actually many different groups of people—already living in the land. In order to establish their own nation, the Israelites engaged in a series of battles against these nations. The Book of Joshua tells the story of many of these battles.

The Israelites were very different from the people who lived around them. The other peoples worshiped many gods, but Israel worshiped only one God, the Lord. Other nations intermarried often and began to worship one another's gods. Israelites preferred to marry within their own community, helping to ensure that their single-hearted worship of God would not be diluted.

The struggles in the land of Canaan did not end with Joshua's death. Israel's history as a nation is full of stories of battles, sieges, and conquests, with towering victories and staggering defeats.

The Question of War

Christians have struggled with questions of war and peace since the earliest years of the Church. It wasn't easy to reconcile the Old Testament's narratives of battles with Jesus' call to be peacemakers (see, for example, Matthew 5:9 and 26:52). Paul and the Book of Revelation recast battling as the fight between good and evil (see Ephesians 6:10–17 and Revelation 12:7–12). Other early Christian writers followed suit, writing important works about the spiritual battle to resist evil and allow the good to triumph. They suggested spiritual disciplines, such as prayer and fasting, to help prepare for spiritual battle, much as a soldier might use physical training to prepare for combat.

The question of participation in military combat remains thorny. At times, Christianity was equated with pacifism, and soldiers had to leave the army before being baptized. (Rather than the morality of participating in wars, this restriction might have been caused by the close ties between service in the Roman army and worship of the Roman gods.) After Christianity became the official religion of the Roman Empire, theologians began to reflect on when force could be used in defense of the nation. The fruit of this reflection is called the "just war" doctrine. This teaching continues to be refined as methods of warcraft and the capabilities of weaponry change. Today, given the use of improvised explosive devices (IEDs), land mines, drones, and similar weapons, some theologians wonder whether the conditions for a just war can ever be met.

Read More About Joshua

Exodus 17, 32
Numbers 11, 13—14
Deuteronomy 34
Joshua
Sirach 46:1–6

Questions to Think About

1. What qualities make a good leader?
2. How do those qualities coexist with the qualities of a good disciple of Christ?
3. What steps can I take to become a person who is better able to follow Christ and lead people to him?

Prayer

Lord,
I want to follow you in everything I do.
Help me to lead with generosity and courage,
keeping your example of loving service always in mind.
May I always lead people to you.
Amen.

Chapter 5

LaShawn: A Real-Life Samuel

Samuel answered, "Speak, for your servant is listening."

1 SAMUEL 3:10

L aShawn was a good learner—and not just in school. In school, he always tried to get a seat in the front of the classroom. He wasn't afraid to ask questions if he didn't understand something. He'd even seek the teacher's help outside the classroom if necessary. He studied and tried to make sure he understood each subject to the best of his ability.

In his part-time job, LaShawn shadowed the manager, taking every opportunity to learn how to do something new—how to fill out a report, repair a malfunctioning piece of equipment, or respond to a customer's question. No one was surprised when LaShawn got promoted.

LaShawn even learned while he was having fun. He listened and watched when the master at his dojo taught a new move. Then he practiced relentlessly until he perfected it.

He paid close attention in his online role-playing game, carefully learning new strategies that made his quests more successful and led him to higher levels. Sure, all that learning was hard work, but when he looked at the results, LaShawn knew it was worth it.

Who Is Samuel?

Samuel was very much a wanted child. His parents, Elkanah and Hannah, had been married a very long time, but seemed unable to have children. Hannah and Elkanah were very faithful to the Lord. On one of their regular visits to the Temple, Hannah prayed fervently for a child, promising God that if she had a son, she would dedicate him to the Lord's service for life. When Samuel was born, she rejoiced in this gift from God.

Hannah remembered her promise to God. When Samuel was a young boy, she took him to the Temple and placed him in the service of Eli, the priest. (Hannah didn't abandon Samuel. She and Elkanah visited him whenever they came to the Temple to pray and offer sacrifice.) Samuel was fortunate to live and work with Eli. Eli was a holy man who was faithful to the Lord. Samuel became his disciple, and Eli led him into a relationship with the Lord.

One of Samuel's duties was to sleep in the Temple. As he slept one night, he heard someone calling his name. Assuming it was Eli, Samuel ran to Eli to see what he needed. Eli responded that he hadn't called Samuel and sent him back to bed. After this happened a few more times, Eli realized that the Lord was calling Samuel. So Eli taught Samuel his most important lesson. He taught Samuel to respond to the Lord with an open heart. Samuel took this good advice and began a lifetime of listening and responding to the Lord with his whole heart. In the years to come, Samuel continued to learn from Eli. Eli treated Samuel as a disciple, helping him learn how to know and love the Lord.

Samuel lived at a time of transition in the land of Israel. For generations, the twelve tribes of Israel had been knit into a loose confederation, with each tribe having its own territory. The people were ruled by judges. These judges didn't preside over court cases the way modern judges do. Instead, they led the people in times of difficulty, especially when Israel was under attack. Samuel served as the last of the judges and the first prophet in the land of Israel.

During Samuel's life, the people of Israel decided they wanted to be like the nations that surrounded them and have a king who would lead them in battle and rule over them. Samuel cautioned the people about the privileges the king would enjoy and the burdens he would impose on the people. But the people refused to budge. So the Lord sent Samuel to anoint his chosen king, a man named Saul.

Once Israel had its king, Samuel's time as a judge ended. But his role as a prophet did not. As the Lord's prophet in the new monarchy, Samuel conveyed the Lord's messages to Saul. In that way, Saul would know how to please the Lord in his actions and decisions. Samuel wasn't afraid to let Saul know what he'd done wrong, either. It must have been frightening to have to admonish the king and tell him to repent, but Samuel did as the Lord asked, serving as the conscience of the king.

Unfortunately, Saul became enamored of his power as king. He even began to ignore the messages that Samuel gave him from the Lord. Instead, Saul decided that, rather than obey these messages, he would decide for himself how best to follow the Lord. Samuel made it clear that God does not desire huge showy gifts. To God, the most treasured gift is the gift of our desire to obey his will.

Since Saul was following his own path away from God, God commissioned Samuel to go out once again to anoint the man that the Lord had chosen to be the next king of Israel. Though he feared being caught by Saul's men (anointing a new king while the current king is still alive can be considered treason), Samuel went to the town of Bethlehem, where he met and anointed David, the new king chosen by God.

What Can Samuel Teach Us?

Though it's tempting to think of Samuel as a kingmaker, in truth, his primary role was as a disciple. A disciple is one who learns at the feet of a master teacher. Early in life, Samuel became the disciple of Eli, the priest. Eli taught Samuel about the ritual sacrifices, how to maintain the Temple, and how to strengthen the relationship between the Israelites and the God who led them from slavery to freedom.

Most importantly, Eli taught Samuel to wait for the word of the Lord with a listening heart. Samuel had to learn to listen for the Lord's voice, and so do we. Our world is full of sounds. Many voices fill our ears and heads. We need to be able to isolate the voice of the Lord from this clamor. The process of listening for and isolating the Lord's voice is called discernment.

The similarity between the words "disciple" and "discernment" show their relationship. Discernment isn't something you do once in your life to identify your vocation or your life's path. Instead, discernment is a daily practice of opening your ears, heart, and will to listen for the Lord's voice. Only by hearing the Lord's voice will we know his will for us and then be able to follow it. Following is a final mark of the disciple. It's not enough simply to map out the path ahead. Day after day, you need to take steps along that path, knowing that you will encounter obstacles and even make a few wrong turns. Despite all the difficulties, you keep listening and keep walking, step by step, until your journey ends in God.

So how do you take the first steps on this journey to God? First, you need to clear a little space in your life for quiet. Quiet time makes it easier to listen for the Lord's voice. It's hard to get away from distractions. You may find that it helps to go someplace alone (perhaps a church or your room) and turn off all electronics. At first, just five minutes will seem like an eternity, but as you grow accustomed to the quiet, you may find that you crave this quiet time and miss it when you don't have it in your schedule. Second, you'll want to find a reliable teacher, perhaps a priest, a man or woman in religious life, or a youth minister. This teacher, often called a spiritual director, may suggest texts for you to read or questions for prayer and reflection. Most important, a reliable teacher can help you learn how to pick the Lord's voice out of the mix.

Living as a disciple takes practice. Each day you have to wake up and decide that you want to follow God's will for you. In the course of your journey, you'll take wrong turns. Everyone does. When that happens, you learn from your mistakes and get back on the right path. One (or more than one) wrong turn doesn't negate your whole journey of discipleship. Sometimes you may feel like you are on a treadmill, walking and walking but getting nowhere. But even when you don't seem to be making any progress, continuing to walk keeps you on the path to God.

Priests, Prophets, and Kings

In the rite of baptism for children, after being baptized with water in the name of the Father and of the Son and of the Holy Spirit, each child is anointed on the crown of the head with sacred chrism (a beautifully scented oil) as a reminder of the call to be priest, prophet, and king. To better understand our baptismal call, we need to understand what priests, prophets, and kings actually do.

In ancient Israel, members of the tribe of Levi served the community as priests, following in the footsteps of Aaron, Moses' brother. The Levites were set apart from the people for the task of offering praise and worship to the Lord. In the Church today, God sets some men apart to be priests to serve the faithful by celebrating the sacraments, teaching the faith, and leading people to God. But even those Christians not called to be ordained as priests exercise the priesthood of the baptized, setting apart time to worship God in the liturgy and sacraments, and by making sacrifices, big and small, in their daily lives.

Contrary to popular opinion, the role of prophets was not to foretell the future. Instead, prophets communicated to the people the word of the Lord. Similarly, our baptism calls us to proclaim the good news of the Lord in all we say and do.

Beginning with Saul, the Israelites had a king to lead them in battle and to govern them in peace. Our baptismal call to be kings doesn't mean that we get to rule over anyone. Rather, it means we are to place our skills and efforts at the service of God's people, especially the most vulnerable and those in greatest need. By doing so, we help to build God's kingdom.

Honest Priests

Samuel grew up assisting the priest Eli in his service at the Temple of the Lord. The Lord's Temple at the time was not a majestic building as we might imagine it today. At the time, the Temple was simply the place where the Ark of the Covenant (containing the tablets of the Ten Commandments) was kept and where people came to offer to the Lord the sacrifices required in the law.

Eli's role as a priest was to offer sacrifices on behalf of the people. To provide for his support, Eli was entitled to receive part of almost every sacrifice. Since the sacrifices typically included animals, oil, and grains, the priests and their families had enough to eat. Eli was an honest priest, taking only his share. His sons, however, were not honest. They took more than their share, extorted bribes, and took advantage of the people who sought their help.

We see a similar contrast between honest and dishonest priests in the New Testament. Zechariah, the father of John the Baptist, was an honest priest, fulfilling his priestly duties with care and reverence and keeping the Lord's commandments. On the other hand, many of the high priests of Jesus' time were dishonest. More concerned with maintaining their status and position than with offering faithful worship to the Lord, they collaborated with the Romans who occupied the land and used their roles to maintain the status quo.

Though God is always good, not everyone who serves him (or claims to serve him) will be. It is important to remember that our faith is in God. It does not rely on human perfection.

Read More About Samuel

1 Samuel 1—12, 16, 25, 28:8–25

Sirach 46:13–20

(Samuel doesn't appear in 2 Samuel, even though it bears his name.)

Questions to Think About

1. How do I learn best: by seeing, hearing, doing, or a combination of these?

2. What opportunities do I have to learn more about my faith?

3. What one thing can I start doing today that would help me apply my best learning skills to learning about God and his Church?

Prayer

Lord,
please fill my mind and my heart
with a desire to learn more about you,
and to know my faith better.
May this learning increase my love for you
and help me to follow you more closely.
Amen.

Chapter 6

Josh: A Real-Life David

I have found David, son of Jesse, a man after my own heart;
he will carry out my every wish.

ACTS 13:22

Josh was a star. Everyone knew it. Whatever he touched seemed to turn to gold. He made all-state his first year on the speech team, and by his junior year he was state champion. He was in the homecoming court and was co-captain of the basketball team. No one was surprised when he was elected class president. Josh was such a great guy that everyone—even teachers and parents—seemed to like him, even admire him.

But then Josh betrayed someone—and everyone who believed in him—and used his influence and popularity for his own gain. People were stunned, disappointed, even a bit angry. How could he be so selfish? How could he take advantage of those who had so much less than he did? How could he care so little about the feelings of others?

Then something *really* amazing happened! Josh said he was sorry. Not the usual "I'm sorry if you feel bad," but a real apology. He took responsibility for the hurt he caused and asked people to forgive him. He realized that his behavior had consequences. He did everything he could to atone for what he had done. He might never be as popular or as influential as he was before, but at least he could look at himself in the mirror again.

Who Is David?

You've probably heard of David, most likely from the story of David and Goliath. Maybe you know he was a king or that he wrote the lyrical poems we call Psalms. But there's a lot more to David. Alongside Abraham and Moses, he's one of the most important figures in the Old Testament. So who was he?

David was the youngest son of a family in Bethlehem. His family owned a flock of sheep, and David was their shepherd, watching over the sheep as they grazed to make sure they had enough to eat and drink and that they weren't carried away by thieves or wild animals. When David was still quite young, likely in his teens, God sent the prophet Samuel to Bethlehem to find a new king. The current king, Saul, wasn't following the Lord's commands, so God was looking for his successor. When Samuel saw David, Samuel knew he was in the presence of God's chosen king. God confirmed this choice, so Samuel anointed David with oil. David was filled with the Lord's Spirit and tried to follow the Lord even more closely.

The strength of the Spirit came in handy when David faced Goliath. At the time, the Israelites were in a war with the Philistines, a powerful tribe who lived nearby. Things weren't going well for the Israelites, but they had one chance left—single combat. Single combat would pit Israel's best soldier against the Philistine's best, one-on-one (sort of the ancient world's version of a steel-cage death match, except the loser really died). Whichever champion won the combat, his army would win the battle. But there was one big problem: The Philistine's champion was a giant and a highly trained warrior. No one from Israel wanted to take him on—except David, a kid with nothing more than a slingshot. But because of the strength of David's conviction and Goliath's over-confidence, David killed Goliath and won the battle for Israel.

As you might expect, this great victory made David very famous and popular. He was even invited to live with the king's family. Saul's son, Jonathan, would become David's best friend, and Saul's daughter, Michal, would become one of David's wives. And they all lived happily ever after, right? Well, not exactly. Saul became jealous of David, seeing him as a threat to Saul's own power. Saul played a lot of dirty tricks on David, even trying to kill him. But God kept David safe through it all. And David, unlike Saul, remained faithful to the Lord's commands. At the time, one of the major duties of a king was to lead troops in battle. Given that Israel was in a near-constant state of war, that was an important job. David served as leader in many battles, sometimes alongside Saul and sometimes against him. In one huge battle against the Philistines, Saul and his sons, including Jonathan, were killed. David was proclaimed king of Israel, fulfilling the anointing of Samuel.

David was a good king, strengthening Israel and giving the people a measure of safety from the enemies who surrounded them. He moved the capital to Jerusalem, a stronghold on the top of a mountain. Showing that the Lord was the true king of Israel, David moved the Ark of the Covenant to Jerusalem, dancing with joy in God's presence, humbling himself before God. The Ark contained the tablets of the Ten Commandments given to Moses. It was a powerful symbol of God's presence among the people of Israel, the people he had chosen to be his own. Because of David's faithfulness, God made a covenant with David, promising that the house of David would last forever (see Psalm 89). This promise was fulfilled in Jesus Christ, of the house of David, who reigns forever.

But David didn't always choose to do what was right. In fact, the course of his life and his family's life were changed by his greatest sin. One evening, while walking around his rooftop patio, he caught sight of a woman named Bathsheba taking a bath, and he decided that he wanted her. It didn't matter to him that she was married. (David was married, too. In fact, he had several wives at the time.) But David wanted what he wanted. The whole thing might have remained hidden, but Bathsheba discovered she was pregnant. How could she explain this pregnancy, given that her husband, Uriah, was a leader in the army and currently deployed away from home? David, eager to cover up his sin, ended up making things worse. He invited Uriah to Jerusalem to report on the war's progress, assuming that while he was there, Uriah would spend time with Bathsheba. Then she could pass the baby off as his. But Uriah refused to sleep with his wife while his men were still in the field. Uriah returned to the field, but David and Bathsheba's problem remained. So David sent a note along with Uriah, ordering the general to start a battle and abandon Uriah on the front lines, a sitting duck certain to be killed. When news of Uriah's death arrived in Jerusalem, David married the new widow and she gave birth to their son.

Greatly displeased by David's behavior, God sent the prophet Nathan to expose David's sin. In this terrible moment, David showed his true strength. He accepted responsibility for his sin and repented in earnest. He didn't avoid blame or make excuses. He admitted that he was wrong and asked God to forgive him (see Psalm 51). David knew that God loved him and wanted to forgive him, so David trusted in the Lord's unfailing mercy. His trust was not in vain.

Though God forgave David completely, everything didn't go back to the way it was before. David's family was never united and loving. The children of his various wives fought with and even killed one another, vying to see who would control the nation after David. Even when David was a very old man, close to death, two of his sons schemed to succeed him as king. Ultimately, the fights between the various factions would continue to haunt Israel for generations.

What Can David Teach Us?

The most important lesson David can teach us is the simple fact that we are all sinners. Each of us, no matter how powerful or how holy, sins. We do things we shouldn't, or we fail to do the things we should. We hurt other people through our selfishness or carelessness. We take the easy way out to save face. We do what is wrong, and we fail to live by God's commandments. But David also teaches us that our sins aren't the end of the story. God is always waiting to forgive us, hoping that we will repent.

But what does it mean to repent? The first step toward repentance is admitting that you sinned and accepting responsibility for your actions. Second, you need to be sorry for your actions, really sorry that you hurt other people and didn't act the way a follower of Christ should act. Third, you need to place your trust in God's mercy, knowing that God will grant forgiveness to those who ask him. Fourth, you need to accept the consequences of your actions. Forgiveness isn't a "get out of jail free" card. You may need to make restitution or take other action to rebuild trust. In some cases, you may never regain the status you once had. Finally, you need to resolve to do better in the future. This resolution isn't a shallow promise to do better next time. It means seriously looking at your own faults and failings and trying to find ways to avoid falling into the same old patterns. You may need to avoid certain temptations, be they people or places. You may need to seek help from a trusted peer or adult who will help you to be accountable. In all cases, you should turn to the Lord in prayer, asking God to give you the strength you need to resist the temptation and to stand up for what is right.

If these steps sound familiar to you, that shouldn't be a surprise. As Catholics, we experience and celebrate these steps in the sacrament of penance. We confess our sins and express contrition (sorrow). The priest assures us of God's mercy and absolves us of our sins. We accept our penance and make a firm resolution to do better in the future with the help of God's grace, continuing our conversion by turning away from sin and toward God.

Going to confession should be a regular part of your life as a believer. Receiving the sacrament of penance isn't a sign of weakness; it's a sign of strength. It takes a strong person, like David, to admit when he or she is wrong. It takes a strong will to change your life, conforming to God's will. It takes strong faith to place your trust in God's mercy.

We should celebrate God's mercy every day. Daily reflection on our merciful and forgiving God will help prepare you to receive the sacrament of penance. Each night, before bed, take a few moments in quiet to think about your day. When did you try to follow God's path? When did you fall short? It might help to read one of the psalms about God's mercy and forgiveness (for example, Psalm 32 or 51). Then, say an act of contrition or use your own words to tell God you're sorry and want to do better. Finish your prayer by thinking about what you can do tomorrow to be a better follower of Jesus. Finally, thank God for his mercy and for the gift of another day. If you place your trust in the Lord like David did, you won't be disappointed.

Psalms

The psalms are a collection of prayerful poetry found in the Bible. The Book of Psalms contains 150 psalms. Many of these prayer-poems are attributed to David.

While all of the psalms touch in some way on our relationship with God, there are many different types of psalms. Some were composed to be sung at royal events, like the coronation or wedding of a king. Others were sung by people on pilgrimage to Jerusalem to celebrate a feast of the Lord. Some provide instruction in how to live a faithful life, or they offer praise to God for his goodness. Still others express very human emotions such as repentance, fear, anger, and abandonment. No matter what the topic, God is at the center of the psalms. God is the source of our strength. He forgives us, comforts us, and protects us.

The psalms have always been an important part of the Church's prayer. Like centuries of Jews before them, Jesus and his apostles prayed the psalms, both alone and together. The early Church continued that practice, praying the psalms throughout the day. Even today, the psalms are an important part of Christian prayer. We pray a psalm during the Liturgy of the Word at every Mass. The psalms are the backbone of the Liturgy of the Hours, prayer prayed throughout the day by clergy and many lay people.

Try praying the psalms yourself:

When you are happy, try Psalm 148.

When you feel alone, try Psalm 22.

When you need help, try Psalm 121.

When you are sorry, try Psalm 130.

When you need to know that God loves you, try Psalm 39.

The language of the psalms is often very emotional, even graphic. While the language may be unfamiliar to you, remember that these prayers show that you can bring anything to God in prayer.

Dysfunctional Families

Most people think their families are weird, but the Bible is full of families that are outright dysfunctional. (Joseph's brothers sold him into slavery!) The story of David highlights two such dysfunctional families: Saul's and David's. Jonathan sided with David against his own father. Michal protected David from Saul's rage but later turned against David, rejecting him completely. David's kids were poster children for dysfunction. Their constant rivalry led to betrayal, rape, exile, and even murder.

The Bible doesn't praise these families or hold them up as examples to be emulated. Instead, these families remind us that God wants to enter into the messiness of our lives. We don't have to be perfect or come from the ideal family. Rather, God waits to receive us as we are. Then, through his grace, bestowed in the sacraments of penance and the Eucharist, he will help us to become the people he calls us to be.

Read More About David

1 Samuel 16–31

2 Samuel (the whole book)

1 Kings 1—2

Questions to Think About

1. Why do I try to avoid blame or responsibility when I've done something wrong?

2. Are there things (people, places, circumstances) that keep me from being a faithful follower of Christ?

3. Do I truly believe that God wants to forgive me? Why or why not?

4. Do I receive the sacrament of penance regularly to receive the gift of God's mercy?

Prayer

Lord,
I know that I don't always live
the way you want me to live.
I do things that hurt myself, you, and others.
Help me to trust in your mercy
and to be truly sorry for my sins
so that I may grow ever closer to you.
Amen.

Chapter 7

Amina: A Real-Life Solomon

I give you a heart so wise and discerning that there has never been anyone like you until now, nor after you will there be anyone to equal you.

1 Kings 3:12

A mina was smart—not just book smart; she was street smart, too. Somehow, she always seemed one step ahead. She was never the person finishing her homework on the bus while texting three friends to make weekend plans. Amina was friendly to everyone, but she knew who her real friends were—the people she could count on when she really needed them. When she was invited to an all-night post-prom party, she thought she'd have to decline. Dawn was way past her curfew. She was surprised when her parents told her she could go and that they trusted her not to do anything risky or stupid. Her dad told her, "Amina, we've known you your whole life. You think about your options, and you make good choices. Why would you stop now?" Knowing that her parents trusted her made Amina feel even better than the party invitation did. Her parents were treating her like an adult!

Who Is Solomon?

Solomon was the son of King David and Bathsheba. (He was actually their second son. The son born of their adultery died shortly after birth.) At Bathsheba's urging, David designated Solomon to succeed him as king of Israel. But his succession wasn't quite as easy as it sounded. Adonijah, one of David's other sons (by a different mother) really wanted to be king—so much so that he tried to establish himself as king before David died. But thanks to Bathsheba's cleverness and the cooperation of David's chief aides, Solomon was anointed king and seated on the throne.

In his final advice to Solomon, David reminded his son of the importance of following the Lord's commandments. As long as Solomon's relationship with God was strong, his kingship and his nation would be secure. Solomon took this advice and was devoted to God. One day, while Solomon was praying, God invited him to ask for a gift. Solomon responded by asking for a heart filled with understanding, so he would know what was right and what was wrong. God was very pleased with this request. Solomon didn't ask for riches or power or something for himself. Solomon asked for a gift that would make him a better king.

God granted Solomon the gift of an understanding heart. Solomon became known throughout Israel and even beyond for his wisdom. Solomon showed great insight into human nature. He was known to be a just judge. People would come to him with their disputes and concerns so he could offer resolutions.

In one famous case recorded in the Bible, two women who shared a house came to him with their dispute. The women had given birth to sons only days apart. One woman's son died during the night, and she substituted her dead baby for the other woman's living child. Since DNA testing didn't exist yet, Solomon needed another way to decide the case. He asked for a sword and said he would cut the child in two, giving half to each woman. One of the women agreed to this division, but the other objected strongly, begging Solomon to give the child to the other woman, thus sparing his life. Solomon gave the living child to the woman who begged for him to be spared, knowing that the child's real mother would place the child's welfare ahead of her own desires.

Because of judgments like these, Solomon's wisdom became famous. Many wise sayings in the Book of Proverbs are attributed to Solomon. The Book of Wisdom includes a lengthy section praising Solomon for his wisdom. As his reputation spread, leaders of other nations visited Israel to consult with Solomon. The Bible recounts one such visit from the Queen of Sheba. Reportedly, after meeting Solomon, she was convinced that no king in the world was wiser and no kingdom was more just or better organized.

Though Solomon did much to secure the borders of Israel and bring it a measure of peace, his greatest achievement was neither military nor political. Solomon built the Temple in Jerusalem. This Temple, built of the best materials and with the finest workmanship, was a visible reminder to the Israelites that their relationship with God was at the center of their existence as a nation. Their power and uniqueness came not from wealth or diplomacy or military prowess, but from their status as the Chosen People of God. The Temple was where the Ark of the Covenant was kept and the place where priests offered sacrifices on behalf of the people. It was a visible reminder that God dwelt with his people.

Unfortunately, Solomon's story does not end happily. He made many political marriages, taking foreign wives to cement strategic alliances. Some of those wives brought with them their worship of foreign gods. Solomon not only created places where they could pray to their gods, he sometimes joined them in their prayers, abandoning his worship of the one true God who had brought the people of Israel out of slavery in Egypt and given them a land of their own. After Solomon's death, the kingdom of Israel would never again be whole. His sons divided the country, and the two parts faced years of conquest and exile. The northern part of the kingdom was ultimately destroyed.

What Can Solomon Teach Us?

Wisdom was valued in Solomon's day, but it's no less valuable today. The ability to assess a situation, to understand people, and to make good decisions are skills that most people strive to develop. These gifts may not be the ones that make us the most popular or give us the money to have all the things we want, but they are essential to living a fulfilling and holy life. Solomon understood that true wisdom is not just a matter of the mind; it is a matter of the heart as well. He asked God to give him an understanding heart so he could be a good king. In the same way, we can never be truly wise if our brains alone control our choices. We must engage our hearts as well.

Even more, as Solomon placed the Temple in the center of Jerusalem, we must keep God at the center of our lives. Only God can give understanding hearts and make us wise. True understanding comes from seeing people as God sees them, and wisdom comes from seeking to know and do God's will. Without God as part of our thinking and feeling, our decisions are far more likely to be founded in selfishness and rash judgment.

We must always remember the warning Solomon provides. Solomon surrounded himself with wives who worshiped foreign gods, and he let himself be influenced by these wives so he, too, began to worship these false gods. From that time on, the kingdom became increasingly unstable, since the king no longer worshiped the Lord alone. We must take care to avoid making friends who will lead us astray and instead surround ourselves with companions who encourage us to be the people God calls us to be. This does not mean we cannot have friends who have different religious beliefs. In fact, having a friend from a different church or even a different faith might encourage us to learn more about our faith so we can answer their questions about what we believe. But a "friend" who dismisses what you believe, jokes about it, or pressures you to change your beliefs is not a friend at all.

Wisdom

Wisdom is an important concept in the Bible. There's even a group of seven biblical books called Wisdom Books (and one of those seven is titled the Book of Wisdom). In biblical terms, wisdom is very different from intelligence. Wisdom doesn't mean that you know a lot of important facts and dates or that you can solve equations or program in the most complex computer languages. Wisdom means you know what you need to know to live a happy, healthy, and holy life.

Often in the Bible, Wisdom is personified as Woman Wisdom, the living opposite of Folly (also personified as a woman). Wisdom throws a large party, inviting everyone she can find to join her, but some choose to join Folly instead. Folly is an unreliable friend, always with you when things are good but nowhere to be found when the going is tough. Wisdom, on the other hand, is a good friend who will bring out your best and never lead you astray.

The Wisdom books of the Bible remind us that the "beginning of wisdom is the fear of the LORD" (Proverbs 9:10). That phrase may be confusing. Why would God want you to be afraid of him? Fear of the Lord doesn't mean being afraid of God. It means being aware of God's power and God's goodness, knowing that God is in charge, not you. Once you understand that basic fact, you are already on your way to being wise.

Good Choices, Bad Choices

Life is all about choices. Our days are filled with choices—from the time we choose to get up to the time we choose to go to bed. Even not making a choice is a choice. Some choices really aren't that important to the big picture of your life. After all, it probably won't make a big difference if you decide to have oatmeal for breakfast instead of yogurt. Other decisions can be life-changing, with good or bad results. Choosing to go on a mission trip could open your eyes to the needs of people in other parts of the world, inspiring you to use your life to make a difference in their lives. On the negative side, choosing to send and receive text messages while you are driving can cause a life-changing (or life-ending) injury for you or someone else.

So what can you do to make better choices? A first step is to surround yourself with friends who make good choices. Friends have a big influence on the decisions we make, so they should be a good influence. You might want to evaluate your options, looking at their pros and cons, their costs and benefits, before deciding. Many people may tell you to ask yourself, "Which choice is best for me?" But your evaluation can't stop there. Every decision you make has a ripple effect in your life and in the lives of others, so you need to ask yourself some other questions as well:

What decision is best for the people around me?

Who will be hurt/helped by the choice I make?

Which choice will bring me closer to the person God wants me to be?

Read More About Solomon

1 Kings 1—11
Proverbs 10—22, 25—29
Wisdom 6:22—11
Sirach 47:12–24

Questions to Think About

1. Do you find it easy or difficult to make choices? Why?

2. What input helps you make decisions?

3. What role does God play in the decisions you make?

Prayer

God,
you are the source of all wisdom.
Fill my heart with understanding
so that I may choose wisely
and follow the path that leads to you.
Amen.

Chapter 8

Miguel: A Real-Life Tobiah

Through all your days, son, keep the Lord in mind, and do not seek to sin or to transgress the commandments. Perform righteous deeds all the days of your life, and do not tread the paths of wickedness.

Tobit 4:5

Miguel lived with his mom, younger brothers and sisters, and his *abuela* in a small rental house in the city. His father had died two years ago after a brief illness. Because he was the oldest, Miguel carried a lot of responsibility. His mom worked long hours at two jobs to provide for the family, so Miguel helped his *abuela* take care of the younger children and the house. He was good at helping the kids with their homework, and he was even learning to cook a little so he could help his *abuela* even more. Maybe when he was a bit older he could get a part-time job after school and reduce the burden on his mom a little bit. By then, his sister, Ana, would be old enough to help more at home.

Sometimes, Miguel felt he was missing out. His friends talked about the shows they watched and the concerts and movies they attended. Cable and movies weren't in Miguel's budget. And even though he was invited to the parties, he couldn't leave *Abuela* without help at home. Helping out was his responsibility. With all of his chores and homework, some weeks the only free time Miguel had was his weekly youth-ministry gathering. His mom made sure she was off that night, because she wanted Miguel to have a good relationship with God and his Church. Miguel liked it, too. He got to spend time with his friends praying and learning—and sometimes just having fun. Most important, Miguel learned how to take his concerns about his life to Jesus. With Jesus helping to carry his burden, it was never too heavy.

Who Is Tobiah?

Tobiah was the son of Tobit and Anna, Jewish exiles living in Nineveh during the Babylonian exile. Tobit was a righteous and holy man, following all of God's commands, even when his neighbors ridiculed and threatened him because of his actions. In addition to the troubles caused by his nasty neighbors, shortly after we meet Tobit in the Bible, he is afflicted with a disease that caused blindness. Things were so bad for Tobit that he asked God to let him die.

Before he died, Tobit wanted to make sure he provided for Anna and Tobiah. Tobit remembered he had deposited a large sum of money with a relative who lived far away. He decided to send Tobiah to get the money and bring it back. Since Tobiah didn't know the way, he went out to find a reliable guide who could make the journey with him. Without Tobiah's knowing it, God sent the angel Raphael in disguise to accompany Tobiah. Together, along with Tobiah's dog, they set off.

During their journey, Tobiah went for a swim, and a large fish attacked him, trying to eat his foot! Tobiah managed to catch the fish and throw it on shore. At Raphael's insistence, Tobiah cut the fish open and removed the internal organs that could be used as medicine—the heart, the liver, and the gall. The rest of the fish became provisions for the journey.

Their journey took them near the home of one of Tobiah's relatives, a man named Raguel who lived with his wife, Edna, and their only child, Sarah. They were a family in crisis. Sarah had been married seven times but, because of the presence of a demon, each of her husbands had died before the couple slept together. Sarah was humiliated by the rumors being spread about her, and she, like Tobit, prayed for death. God had sent Raphael to help her, too.

At this time in history, people typically married within their own tribe or clan. Thus, Tobiah had the right to marry Sarah if he wanted. He decided he wanted to do so, even after being warned about the fate of her past husbands. Sarah gave her consent and they were married. Before going to bed, Tobiah burned the fish's heart and liver so that the smoke (and, one assumes, the smell) would drive the demon away. Then Tobiah and Sarah began their married life by praying together. Because of God's intervention, Tobiah survived until morning, and he and Sarah began their long and happy marriage.

Raguel and Edna planned a large wedding celebration. Before the celebration began, Tobiah sent Raphael to get the money that Tobit had left on deposit. Then, the fourteen-day wedding celebration began! At the end of the celebration, Tobiah and Sarah started their journey back to Nineveh accompanied by Raphael and generous wedding gifts from Sarah's parents.

Because Tobiah had been gone longer than expected, his parents feared he had had an accident on the way. But at last, Tobiah returned home, to his parents' great joy. Not only had he brought Tobit's money, he'd brought them a new daughter-in-law. Even more, the gall he had saved from the fish attack was the medicine needed to cure Tobit's blindness. In joy over the blessings that had come to his family, Tobit gave Raphael half the money he had brought back as a (huge!) bonus for his good work.

At this point, Raphael revealed he was an angel sent by God to answer the prayers of Tobit and Sarah. He reminded Tobit and

Tobiah of the importance of remaining faithful to the Lord and turning to God in prayer. Then, Raphael disappeared. Tobiah and Sarah lived with Tobit and Anna, raising their seven sons. After Tobit and Anna died, Tobiah and Sarah and their family returned to her parents' home where they cared for Raguel and Edna. Through all these years, they remained faithful to the Lord.

What Can Tobiah Teach Us?

Though his circumstances are very unfamiliar to us, we can draw two important lessons from Tobiah's story. First, Tobiah demonstrates the importance of honoring (obeying and respecting) one's parents. Tobiah learned how to live a good and virtuous life by watching his father. He listened to his father's advice and instructions and did his best to follow them. Even when his father asked him to undertake a difficult journey, Tobiah agreed to do it without complaint. Tobiah showed concern for his parents, knowing they would be very worried by his delayed return. Then he, along with Sarah, cared for his parents and hers in their old age.

Maintaining a good relationship with your parents can be very difficult. It may seem as though they don't understand the challenges you face, and their advice may seem hopelessly out of date. Should you really take life advice from people who need your help every time they need to download an app to their phones? The first step in developing a good relationship is realizing that, in the course of their lives, your parents have faced many of the same struggles and felt the same confusing emotions as you do. While their experiences may not be exactly the same as yours, their experience can still be helpful. Your parents can help you identify new options and see past your immediate concerns.

As Tobiah demonstrates, respect for your parents doesn't end when you turn eighteen or get your first job or even when you marry and have kids of your own. Our parents deserve our respect all their lives. As they grow older, the tables may be turned. They may need our help and advice, care, and nurturing.

The second thing Tobiah's story can teach us is that no problem is beyond God's help. Both Tobit and Sarah, overwhelmed by their problems, prayed to God for death, but God knew their problems could be overcome. God sent Raphael to help Tobiah resolve Tobit and Sarah's problems. When you feel as though your problems are insurmountable and that you'd be better off dead, you can always take your problems to God in prayer. And then you can turn to the trusted people around you—a priest or youth minister, a teacher or school counselor, even a doctor—to see who might help you find your angel in disguise.

Marriage

Tobiah's marriage to Sarah is the heart of the Book of Tobit. Tobiah and Sarah didn't date for years and have a big wedding. In fact, they married the same day they met (though they did have quite the wedding feast!). Still, the Book of Tobit tells us they had a long and happy marriage.

Wedding customs have certainly changed since Tobiah's day, but some things have remained unchanged. First, Tobiah and Sarah could follow the examples of the loving marriages of their parents, Tobit and Anna, and Raguel and Edna. Though these couples faced prosperity and hardship, joy and arguments, they loved each other and remained faithful to each other. By watching their parents over the years, Tobiah and Sarah learned what married love is like. Many young people today cannot look to their parents' example of a loving, happy marriage. If that is your case, you might want to find an older married couple in your parish or neighborhood who can play that role for you.

Tobiah and Sarah did one other thing that made their marriage a success. They kept God at the center of their relationship with each other. The very first thing they did as a married couple was to pray together. Keeping God as their firm center—through prayer, worship, and living justly—they grew closer to each other.

Prayer, Fasting, and Almsgiving: Holy Living

Throughout his life, Tobit gave his son, Tobiah, a lot of good advice. Most of that advice on how to live a holy life still applies today.

Tobit taught his son to turn to God in prayer every day. He told Tobiah to thank the Lord for all the blessings of his life, to seek comfort in times of sorrow, and to ask for advice and counsel when making decisions. (You can see some of Tobit's prayers in Tobit 3:2–6 and Tobit 13:1–18.)

Tobit told Tobiah to be willing to share his food, clothing, and money with those in need. He said Tobiah should give to the needy even if he didn't have much himself. Rather than acquiring more and more, Tobiah should fast from time to time so his sacrifice would allow others to have what they need. The practice of giving from your own possessions to those in need is called almsgiving. Almsgiving remains an important practice today, when so many of our brothers and sisters lack even the basic necessities of life.

Finally, Tobit counseled Tobiah to treat others justly, paying workers fairly and treating everyone with dignity and respect.

Read More About Tobiah

Book of Tobit, especially chapters 4—12

Questions to Think About

1. How do you show respect for your parents and others in authority?
2. How can you tell if a friend is a faithful companion who will help you live according to God's will?
3. What can you do today that will help you live a holier life?

Prayer

Lord,
help me to be like Tobiah,
respecting and obeying those in authority
and sharing my journey with those who will guide me to you.
May I always be willing to listen
to the good advice of my elders
and bring my concerns to you in prayer.
Amen.

Chapter 9

Delanie: A Real-Life Esther

My Lord, you alone are our King. Help me, who am alone and have no help but you, for I am taking my life in my hand.

Esther C:14–15

Delanie was excited—and scared. She had the opportunity to be part of a special youth mission trip sponsored by her church. First, she would go to Italy for two weeks to train and plan with other members of the international team. Then they'd all fly to Africa for two months of work building a school and staffing a clinic.

Delanie really wanted to go, but she was nervous. She'd never been outside the country before. She wouldn't know anyone else on the trip. The other team members might speak languages she didn't understand. The food and climate would be different from those at home. Delanie would miss the summer with her friends, and she'd likely find the heat, the bugs, and the simple living conditions uncomfortable. Her parents helped her think through her options and told her they would support any decision she made. But the final decision was Delanie's. Should she go, or should she stay home? There was only one thing she could do. She prayed: "God, I'm scared and I don't know what to do. Please help me to have the courage to do what you want me to do. Be my strength."

Who Is Esther?

It all started with a wild party. The king of Persia threw a huge party for his male friends. (The queen partied separately with the other women.) The king decided it would be a good idea to show off his beautiful wife to his drunken party guests. When the queen refused to appear, the king was angry and embarrassed. His advisors had a plan, though. The king should discard the old queen and find a new one.

The king liked this plan and announced that the most beautiful young women in the kingdom would be gathered into the palace. There, they would spend a full year getting beauty treatments. After this time of preparation, each young woman would go to the king. The king would choose the one he liked best to be his new queen. The rest would become his concubines, joining his harem.

One of the young women who moved to the palace was a Jewish orphan named Esther. She lived with her Uncle Mordecai, who had adopted her as his own. Soon after Esther moved into the palace, she became a favorite of the man in charge of the "contestants" for the role of queen. She took his advice and learned everything she could to please the king. When it was her turn to go to the king, the king was so pleased with her that he made Esther his queen.

Esther's uncle was in service to the king. Because of his excellent service, Mordecai was given promotions and honors—plus he could keep an eye on Esther. Unfortunately, Mordecai's success aroused the jealousy of Haman, another man serving at court. In addition to being jealous, Haman was angry that Mordecai refused to give him traditional signs of respect, such as bowing. (Jews did not bow before any human being. They reserved such signs for God alone.) Haman decided to get rid of all the Jews, including Mordecai. At the time, no one knew that Queen Esther was Jewish. Playing on the king's fears of rebellion, Haman convinced him to authorize a letter calling for the murder of all Jews throughout the kingdom. As soon as Mordecai learned about the plan, he sent a message to Esther, begging her to help. Esther faced a tough situation. According to the customs of the time, Esther wasn't allowed to visit the king without an invitation. Entering the king's presence uninvited was a crime punishable by death. The king could, however, choose to spare the intruder. Still, if Esther decided to approach the king, she'd be gambling with her life.

Esther did the only thing she could do—she prayed that God would grant her courage and guide her actions. She behaved like a person in mourning, giving up all the luxuries she enjoyed as queen, praying intensely for three days. At the end of the three days, she dressed in her best queenly attire and approached the king. She had to lean on her maids because she was so weakened by her three days of prayer and fasting. At first, the king was very angry that she had come to him uninvited. But moved by seeing her weakness, he welcomed her and spared her life. Esther responded by inviting the king and Haman to a banquet she would throw. At this banquet, the king told Esther to ask for anything she wanted. She asked the king and Haman to come to a second banquet.

At the second banquet, the king again invited Esther to ask for whatever she wanted. This time, Esther begged the king to save her life and the lives of her people, revealing to him that she was Jewish and informing him of the details of Haman's plot. Angered by Haman's actions, the king left the banquet and walked in the garden to blow off steam. While the king was gone, knowing his life was in jeopardy because of the king's anger, Haman begged Esther to spare his life, throwing himself on the couch where Esther was lying. (At this time, people ate banquets while reclining on couches.) The king came back into the banquet room and saw Haman seeming to lie on the queen. Needless to say, this sight made the king even angrier, sealing Haman's fate.

Of course, Haman's death didn't solve the Jews' problem. The decree calling for their murder had been issued already. To save the Jews, the king gave Mordecai permission to issue a new letter in the king's name, allowing the Jews to arm themselves and fight back. Thus, Queen Esther saved the Jewish community in Persia, a victory that Jews today still celebrate on the feast of Purim.

What Can Esther Teach Us?

While most of us will never hold the fate of a people in our hands, we can still learn from Esther. First, she teaches us we need to have the courage to look beyond our own safety and do whatever we can to promote the common good. For us, the opportunities to serve the common good may be less dramatic than Esther's, but that doesn't mean they won't take courage. It takes courage to stand up to bullying, to hold on to your values when your peers may not share them, to refuse to sit by idly when people exhibit prejudice, or treat others as though they don't matter. Each day we face opportunities to do what is right or what is easy. Choosing to do what is right takes courage.

Second, Esther teaches us that the courage we need is founded in our relationship with God. We need to follow Esther's example of praying that we will have courage to take action when necessary. Esther's example of getting rid of her luxuries is instructive as well. When we are surrounded by comfort and excess, it's hard to focus on more important things. They can cloud our judgment with the fear that our courageous actions may place our own comforts at risk. A time of fasting from these distractions can help us find the courage we need to live what we believe.

The Difference Between Protestant and Catholic Bibles

If you decided to read the Book of Esther, you might have noticed it has chapters labeled with letters rather than numbers. You might also notice that the text of this book in your Catholic Bible is different from the text in the Bibles of your Jewish and Protestant friends. To understand the reasons for these differences, you need to understand a bit of history.

In the years before the birth of Jesus, the region where the Israelites lived was conquered by the Greeks. As the Greeks occupied the area, their language and culture grew in influence there. After a while, many Jews spoke Greek, even more than Hebrew. So that these Jews could understand their sacred writings, the Scriptures were translated into Greek. This Greek translation is called the Septuagint.

Similarly, most early Christians spoke Greek. Not surprisingly, these Greek-speaking Christians used the Greek text of the Old Testament. The books of the New Testament were written mostly in Greek.

The Greek text of the Old Testament has several differences from the Hebrew edition. The Septuagint includes seven books omitted from the Hebrew edition: Tobit, Judith, 1 and 2 Maccabees, Wisdom, Sirach (sometimes called Ecclesiasticus or the Wisdom of Ben Sira), and Baruch. The Septuagint includes additions to the Books of Esther and Daniel as well. In Esther, these additions are labeled with letters rather than numbers and placed where they belong throughout the text.

In the first century after Jesus' birth, the Jewish community decided they did not consider the seven books and the additions found only in the Septuagint as part of their sacred Scriptures.

During the Reformation, Protestant communities decided to follow the Jewish example in omitting these texts. The Catholic Church, however, has always considered these books to be inspired by the Holy Spirit and has used them in worship and teaching. These books are sometimes called the deuterocanonical books.

The Weak Prevail

The Bible is filled with stories of the unexpected—an elderly couple has a child, the younger son founds a dynasty, a shepherd boy wins a fight with a seasoned soldier, a virgin bears a child, a dead man comes back to life. A constantly recurring theme throughout the Bible is that, against all odds, the weak prevail. This theme plays out in the story of Esther, where a Jewish orphan becomes a queen capable of saving her people. In the New Testament, Jesus takes this theme a step further, amazing his disciples by teaching that the poor, outcast, and childlike have God's special favor.

This attitude contrasts strikingly with the attitudes most prevalent in our world today. All too often, we seem to revere power, wealth, and fame, using our time and best efforts to acquire them. These efforts may damage our relationships with our families, friends, and God. The stories of the Bible remind us that God plays by different rules. Following the world's rules may get us a nice house, a fancy car, and a good job, but following God's rules can help us live with God in heaven forever. Which rules will you play by?

Read More About Esther

Book of Esther

Questions to Think About

1. Do I follow Esther's lead and take advice from people who are older and wiser?
2. What challenges in my life or faith do I need courage to face?
3. What actions do I take to help those who are weak and struggling?

Prayer

God,
as Esther turned to you in prayer,
I come to you in prayer to ask you to strengthen me
and fill me with the courage I need
to live the way you want me to live,
doing what is right and not just what is easy.
Amen.

Chapter 10

Jessica, Beth, and Amber:
Real-Life Seven Brothers

One of the brothers, speaking for the others, said: "What do you expect to learn by questioning us? We are ready to die rather than transgress the laws of our ancestors."

2 MACCABEES 7:2

Jessica, Beth, and Amber had met in the religion class that prepared them for their first holy Communion, and they had been best friends ever since. They had attended religious-education classes together and now participated in youth ministry. Next summer, they planned to go on the parish's mission trip to help build a catechetical center in El Salvador.

The girls were friends outside of church, too. They studied together after school and did things together almost every weekend. Jessica and Amber attended all of Beth's soccer games, and Beth returned the favor, coming to Amber and Jessica's plays and concerts.

Still, their faith was at the heart of their friendship. It really helped them to talk to one another when they had questions or doubts. When any one of them had a tough decision to make, the other two helped her to discern what God would want. They talked about what they read in the Bible and even prayed for one another. They were sisters in faith.

Who Are the Seven Brothers?

In the years after Alexander the Great, descendants of his Greek troops established control over Israel. This period is called the Seleucid dynasty, or the Hellenistic period. As part of their effort to establish control over the region, they imposed Greek culture, including institutions like the gymnasium and worship of the Greek gods. They placed a statue, probably of Zeus, in the Temple, turning its precincts over to all forms of pagan worship. Finally, the Seleucids made it illegal to practice the Jewish faith. Scrolls of the Law (the Torah) were banned. Mothers who had their sons circumcised in accord with God's command were executed, along with their infants. Many of the people living in Jerusalem, including many leaders and priests, abandoned worship of the Lord and participated in pagan worship. The people who did not accept the forced Hellenization faced enormous hardships. Many of them were tortured and executed, often in horrific ways.

Among these heroes and martyrs were a mother and her seven sons. They were arrested, brought before the king, and asked to demonstrate that they had abandoned their faith by eating pork, a forbidden food. When they refused to eat, they were tortured in increasingly horrible ways. (You do NOT want to read the account of their martyrdom before you eat.) The torture began with scourging and proceeded to maiming and mutilation. Ultimately, if they refused to abandon their faith, they would be killed by being burned alive in a giant frying pan. One brother at a time suffered torture and execution while his brothers and mother watched. The remaining brothers knew the fate that awaited them if they held on to their faith in the Lord. Despite the fear they must have felt, and knowing they could end the pain with a simple bite, they remained faithful. Even more than that, they encouraged one another to stay faithful to the Lord.

Eventually, the king realized his threats of pain and death were ineffective, so he changed tactics with the last brother. The king offered the seventh son power and wealth if he would abandon his faith. In addition, the king tried to convince the mother, who had watched six sons die horribly before her eyes, to save her youngest (and final) son. Imagine the king's surprise when the mother instead urged her son to hold on to his faith and let go of his life on earth, trusting that he would live with God forever in heaven. The seventh son showed his bravery and strength of faith by not only rejecting the king's bribes and accepting painful death, but by stating clearly his trust in God and his belief that he and his brothers would be reunited to live with God forever.

Finally, we must think of the mother who had watched all of her children tortured and murdered before her eyes. Though her heart must have been breaking and her grief overwhelming, she had encouraged her sons to stay strong in faith. She reminded them of the sacrifices she had made to raise them. She encouraged her sons to focus on their life in God rather than their life on earth.

What Can the Seven Brothers Teach Us?

The story of the seven brothers is not for the faint of heart or those weak in faith. These brothers faced great fear and pain, all because of what they believed. At any moment they could have ended their pain and suffering by rejecting their faith and taking a bite of pork. It seems like such a small thing in exchange for saving their lives. So why didn't they follow the example of so many people around them and abandon their faith?

Often, we face challenges to our faith, though they aren't usually matters of life or death. We may be asked to deny our faith in small ways by what we say and do. For example, we may deny our faith by skipping Mass on Sunday to go shopping with friends or deny our values in order to avoid teasing or ridicule. How can the example of the seven brothers help us in these instances?

First, the brothers show us the importance of living one's faith within the family. A family that shares faith at home will be stronger in their practice of the faith. Sharing faith as a family can begin simply by saying grace before meals and attending Sunday Mass together. The Church provides blessings for many events of family life, from birthdays to holidays to times of grief. Families can read the Bible together and discuss what happens and what we can learn from each passage we've read.

Second, the seven brothers demonstrate the importance of having a faith support group. These people may or may not be family members. The key is that they share your faith and will support you in learning and living your faith day by day. As the brothers encouraged one another in the face of the king's tortures, your faith support group will encourage you when your faith is challenged or when you feel overwhelmed by doubt. Members of your support group don't need to be saints. They should be people who struggle with being faithful, just like you do. By giving one another support, and receiving it when necessary, each person's faith will grow stronger.

Finally, the brothers teach us the importance of keeping your eyes on your ultimate goal. The brothers rejected wealth and power—and even living peaceful and undisturbed lives—in favor of their hope of eternal life with God. In the same way, we need to focus on our relationship with Jesus Christ, a relationship that will lead us to eternal life. Nothing else—not friends or money or popularity or success—should distract us from our love for Jesus and our desire to live as he taught.

Who Are the Maccabees?

The name "Maccabees" may come from the Hebrew word meaning "hammer." It comes from the nickname given to Judas, a member of a priestly family during a very difficult time in Israel's history. Israel had been conquered by a dynasty related to Greece, the Seleucid dynasty. The dynastic leaders in Israel tried to stamp out the religion and culture of the Jewish people. Greek institutions replaced the traditional Jewish ones, and it became illegal to practice the Jewish faith. A statue of a Greek god was placed in the Temple of the Lord, and Jews were compelled to offer sacrifice to pagan gods.

Judas, members of his family, and other people opposed the occupation and the suppression of their faith strongly, even violently. They killed people who complied with the demands to offer pagan sacrifices and destroyed the altars to pagan gods. They had great success, even removing the statue from the Temple and returning the Temple to the worship of the Lord. In time, they were able to reestablish Jewish rule over Israel.

Hanukkah

During the time when the Seleucid dynasty controlled Israel, they desecrated the sacred space of the Temple with pagan worship, rendering it unfit for the worship of the Lord.

After the Maccabees regained control of Jerusalem, they cleansed the Temple from all of the pagan influences and once again offered sacrifice to the Lord. The Maccabees and other faithful Jews celebrated the rededication of the Temple for eight days. They decreed that future generations should celebrate this victory and rededication to the worship of the Lord every year, This eight-day celebration is called Hanukkah.

Read More About the Seven Brothers

2 Maccabees 7

Questions to Think About

1. What challenges to your faith do you struggle with the most?

2. Who in your life supports you in learning and living your faith?

3. How do you support others in their faith?

Prayer

God,
thank you for all of the people you have put in my life
who help me to know you better.
Please give me the strength and humility
to turn to them for help when I need it.
Amen.

Chapter 11

Danny: A Real-Life Jeremiah

Do not say, "I am too young."
To whomever I send you, you shall go.

JEREMIAH 1:7

From the time he was in grade school, Danny had a feeling that God had something special planned for him. As soon as he was old enough, he signed up to be an altar server. Even though he hated getting up for the early Mass, he always felt that helping the priest at Mass was the best part of his week. Once he got to high school, he became active in youth ministry, participating in the hour of adoration, service projects, and retreats.

Danny wasn't a perfect kid. Lots of days, he forgot to pray until it was really late and he was already falling asleep. He didn't always do his chores or his homework because, let's face it, mowing the lawn and writing essays isn't as much fun as playing games on the tablet. And if his little brother messed with his stuff one more time, Danny might just disown him for good. But despite his faults, Danny did try to be a good person.

When Danny was a junior, a teacher asked him if he'd ever thought about becoming a priest. Danny's first thought was, "No way! I'm not holy. And I just started dating. No way I'm giving that up!" Even though Danny dismissed the suggestion, the idea just wouldn't go away. He decided to go on a diocesan retreat for young men thinking about becoming priests. The more he thought about the idea, the more he felt that being a priest might be God's plan for him. Once it got around school that he'd gone on the retreat, the other guys started teasing him. Then the girls started asking if he just didn't like girls. Danny hated the teasing and tried to ignore it. Every time he thought about being a priest, he was nervous at first, but then he felt a deep peace.

Danny didn't know if he had what it takes to serve God's people as a priest. He wasn't sure he wanted to live without a wife and family. He knew it would be really hard to put others before himself all the time. But he knew he had to give it his best shot.

Who Is Jeremiah?

At his first appearance in the Bible, Jeremiah was a young man from a family of priests, living in a town near Jerusalem. Then God called him to be a prophet. God had chosen Jeremiah to be a prophet even before he was born. Jeremiah was very uncertain about his call. Immediately, he began to make excuses: He was too young, he wasn't a good speaker, he wouldn't know what to say. God promised Jeremiah that he would help him and tell him what to say and do. So, finally accepting his call, Jeremiah became a prophet and went to Jerusalem.

At the time, things in Jerusalem were pretty bad. The people were no longer worshiping the Lord alone. Instead, they were offering sacrifices to foreign gods and engaging in other practices forbidden by the Lord's commandments. In the early years of Jeremiah's career as a prophet, King Josiah tried to steer the kingdom back on to the right path, but those efforts ended when Josiah died in battle. Soon after his death, things in Israel got even worse. The people fell further and further away from the worship of the Lord, and their security from foreign enemies began to crumble.

As promised, God told Jeremiah what to say and do in his

prophetic preaching. Jeremiah preached several sermons charging Israel with violating the covenant and warning them of the consequences if they did not change their ways. Jeremiah preached throughout Jerusalem, even at the gates of the Temple. In his preaching, Jeremiah used many vivid images and symbolic actions, like parading around wearing a yoke to warn people about the yoke of slavery they would have to carry if they were conquered by a neighboring nation. The Israelites got a first taste of this slavery when a group of civic leaders were sent into exile in Babylon. Though he stayed in Jerusalem, Jeremiah sent the exiles a letter of support, reminding them that God would not abandon them.

As you might imagine, Jeremiah's preaching was not terribly popular with the people of Jerusalem. It's hard to hear someone point out everything you are doing wrong, especially when it's true! The people, especially the leaders who were responsible for what was happening, blamed the messenger—Jeremiah. Jeremiah was punished in many ways, including being threatened, whipped, placed in the stocks, imprisoned, thrown into a cistern and left to die, and forced into exile in Egypt.

Because Jeremiah's life was so difficult, it's not surprising that he often became depressed and discouraged about his ministry as a prophet. He asked God why he'd been given this ministry, even claiming that God had tricked him, although Jeremiah had agreed to become a prophet. Yet, in spite of it all, Jeremiah could not abandon his call. The need to do God's work in the world burned inside him.

Not all of Jeremiah's preaching was filled with condemnation and gloom. As the Israelites were driven into exile, Jeremiah spoke words of comfort, letting them know that God would never abandon them and that God would fulfill his promise and bring them back to their land. God even promised that he would give the people a new covenant, one that would never end. This covenant was fulfilled in the saving death and resurrection of Jesus Christ.

What Can Jeremiah Teach Us?

The first thing Jeremiah teaches us is that God has a plan for each person, no matter how young or how old. We can choose to obey God's will, or we can close our ears and hearts to his call. Still, our truest happiness and peace will come if we follow the path that the Lord sets before us, remaining faithful to his call. Like Jeremiah, we are assured that God will give us what we need to fulfill his call.

Jeremiah also teaches us that living according to God's plan won't always be easy. Sometimes it will be very difficult. We may be ridiculed or even abandoned by people we thought were friends. We may feel discouraged and as though we aren't making a positive impact. We may even begin to think that God has abandoned or tricked us. Having these feelings doesn't mean we are bad people or that we have lost our faith. Still, like Jeremiah, we must remain faithful, knowing God is always there to support us, help us along the way, and bring us to the ultimate happiness that is our destination and the blessing of fidelity.

Living as a Refugee

During Jeremiah's life, the people of Israel were sent into exile in Babylon. When Jerusalem was conquered, much of the city was destroyed. The leading citizens—at least those not killed in the fighting or executed by the conquerors—were forcibly relocated to Babylon. They lost their homes, most of their possessions, their livelihoods, and their heritage. They were forced to live in a new country with a new language, new customs, and new gods. In that challenging environment, they struggled to maintain their identity, their culture, and their relationship with God. (The people who stayed in Jerusalem didn't get off easy. They suffered famine and extreme poverty.)

Exile was particularly difficult for the Israelites because they understood the land as a lasting sign of the covenant and of their status as God's Chosen People. Being separated from the land was a painful reminder that they had failed to keep the covenant by worshiping other gods rather than being faithful to the one true God. Each day of their lives in exile reminded them of their failure.

In our world today, many people are displaced, living as refugees. They have been driven from their homes by war or famine. Many live in camps where disease and crime are rampant. Stays in these "temporary" camps can last years. A large number of these people will never be able to return to their homes. They will be forced to build new lives in new places with new languages and new customs. In some places, they may be treated with scorn or even violence. As people of faith, we must do all we can to help these people feel safe and welcome in their homes.

Symbolic Actions

A saying goes that actions speak louder than words. These words are even truer when it comes to symbolic actions, such as those Jeremiah used. He used symbolic actions to teach about God's relationship with his people. These actions were far more vivid than preaching alone. In addition to teaching with symbolic actions, Jeremiah learned from them as well. Using the example of a potter at the wheel (see Jeremiah 18:1–12), God showed Jeremiah how he would continue to reshape the people of Israel each time they failed.

You may have heard people dismiss something by saying it's

"just a symbol." But symbols are important ways to share meaning. They point to a deeper reality. For example, when Americans salute the flag, they are not honoring a brightly colored piece of cloth, but the nation it represents. Symbols may help people understand a difficult concept or grasp that concept more fully. Jeremiah's smashing a clay flask in front of the people was a powerful way to show what would happen to the nation if they continued to worship false gods. Just as Jeremiah smashed the flask, the Babylonians would smash Israel into pieces, destroying the buildings, trampling the fields, and dispersing the people. Though Jeremiah's sermons said the same thing, the sound and sight of a smashed flask caught the people's attention far more effectively.

Covenant

On the surface, a covenant might seem like a contract: Party 1 will do X (say, mow the lawn) if Party 2 does Y (pays $25). But a biblical covenant is more than that. It is a sacred promise between God and people. Even though we may fail and break our promises, God never will. God will always be faithful.

The Old Testament tells us of several covenants. God promises Noah that he will never again destroy all life on earth. God makes a covenant with Abraham as well, promising that he will be the father of many nations. Abraham and his male descendants mark this covenant with circumcision. In the covenant with Moses, God calls the children of Israel to be his Chosen People, and they agree to follow the laws he has given them. God promises David that his family will always be kings—his throne would be secure forever.

The prophet Jeremiah speaks of a new covenant, one written on our hearts. We won't have to learn how to follow God. We will be so close to God that we will follow him by following our hearts. This covenant was fulfilled in Jesus Christ, who sealed a new covenant in his blood (see Luke 22:20). He became human and, by his death and resurrection, opened the gates of heaven so we might live with God for all eternity. That promise never ends.

Read More About Jeremiah

Book of Jeremiah

Questions to Think About

1. How often do you think about what God wants to do in and through you?

2. How does God's plan for you affect how you live your life each day, as well as your plans for the future?

3. Have you ever felt as though God was asking too much of you? How did you respond?

Prayer

God,
I don't always know what you want from me.
Help me to know and follow your will in everything I do.
Even when things get difficult,
give me strength so I can be faithful to your call.
Amen.

Chapter 12

Noah: A Real-Life Daniel

God stirred up the holy spirit of a young boy named Daniel.

DANIEL 13:45

A n invitation to a party is a good thing, right? Especially when
it comes from one of the most popular kids in school. But
Noah wasn't so sure. Even though he'd only been at the school
for a few months, he'd heard about these parties—and he'd seen
the photos online. There always seemed to be a lot of drinking
(and sometimes more), and lots of couples seemed to disappear
for a while. Noah didn't do any of those things. He didn't believe
that behaving that way was what God wanted from him. But if
he declined the party invitation, he might never get another one.
How would he make friends in the new school? What if they asked
why he couldn't come? Should he lie and say he had other plans?
If he told the truth, he'd be labeled a stiff or a prude—just what
the "new kid" needed! Would he ever fit in? Did he even want to?

Who Is Daniel?

Daniel has an entire book of the Bible named after him, though
he didn't write it. He lived in the city of Babylon about 600 years
before Jesus was born. Daniel was Jewish, not Babylonian, and he
didn't go to Babylon voluntarily. He was in exile. When Judah (the
Jewish nation with its capital in Jerusalem) fell to the Babylonian
army, many of the leading citizens were taken to Babylon to live,
displaced from their homes, property, and livelihoods.

The king of Babylon, Nebuchadnezzar, made a political decision to try to assimilate some of the young people into the Babylonian society so they would grow to be good citizens. He had his officials select a group of promising young men from among the exiles. These young men would be raised in the royal household. The idea was that, after a period of training, the best of these young men would get jobs in the government and become good, loyal Babylonians.

Daniel was one of the young men selected. When he got to the palace, he and some of his friends learned they would receive food and wine from the royal table. Eating this food would violate the Jewish kosher laws, which dictated which foods could and could not be eaten. Rather than violate God's law, Daniel and his friends asked to have the royal food and wine replaced with vegetables and water. The man charged with caring for the young men was worried that the change in diet would make the Israelites look sickly compared to the others who were eating far richer food, but he agreed to try it for ten days. At the end of the trial, Daniel and his friends looked healthier than the other young men in the training program. Daniel and his friends excelled in their studies and, at the end of the training, were selected to enter the king's service.

Daniel's time serving the king included its own challenges. Daniel was skilled at interpreting dreams. Being able to interpret dreams and other signs was a useful skill in government. At this time, the interpretation of dreams was very important because people, including rulers, believed that dreams told them what they should do. As we might use economic forecasting or other political modeling, ancient rulers used dreams and other signs. The various kings of Babylon often asked Daniel to interpret their dreams. Of course, Daniel was able to do this. That wasn't the problem. The problem was that the dreams and signs Daniel had to interpret were not good news for Babylon. Everything Daniel was asked to interpret foretold Babylon's decline and eventual fall. Imagine having to tell the king that his empire was on its way out! It certainly wouldn't make you very popular, and it could actually put your life in danger. Daniel could have taken the easy way out and told the king what he wanted to hear. People tend not to get angry with people who give them good news, but Daniel told the truth, even though it angered the king.

Daniel also resisted the other temptations that came with his skills and his position. He could have used them to increase his own power and wealth. Instead, he remained true to his faith. He understood that power and wealth don't matter in God's eyes. Truth and remaining faithful to the Lord are what matter.

Daniel was always faithful to the Lord, even when it was very difficult. At one point, King Darius (who succeeded the Babylonian king) had decreed that no one could pray to any god except him. In many ancient societies, the king was considered divine. Daniel refused to follow this law, continuing to pray to the Lord. Even though Darius liked Daniel and had entrusted him with much authority, Darius had to follow the law and punish Daniel. The prescribed punishment for violating this law was being cast into a den of lions. Obviously, no one would survive this punishment. But Daniel did. Because Daniel was faithful to the Lord, the Lord closed the lion's mouths and kept them from harming Daniel. Darius was so impressed that he issued a proclamation praising the Lord! Daniel's faithfulness had helped Darius see God's power.

What Can Daniel Teach Us?

It's often easy to go along with the crowd and just ride the current. Daniel teaches us the importance of holding on to our beliefs and being true to ourselves and to our God. Daniel managed to live in Babylon with all of its temptations, yet he remained true to himself. It would have been very easy for him to be seduced by the luxury and power of the royal court and to use his gifts to advance his own interests.

Even though Daniel was dealing with a royal court that believed in governing by the interpretation of dreams, his story still resonates today. In the face of social and academic pressures, it seems so much easier to do what everyone else is doing, even if you know it's wrong. Cheating on a test, buying a paper from a website, forging a parent's signature on a school report, taking the beer you're handed at a party. In times of stress and confusion, any of those things may seem like an easy way to avoid conflict. You never have to explain to people why you're doing what everyone else is doing. They already know. It's so much harder to explain why you are doing what you think is right: taking a bad grade because you haven't studied, giving up a fun event to finish a project, facing an angry and disappointed parent, accepting teasing because you don't drink.

Daniel reminds us of the importance of holding tightly to your values. A person without a strong foundation is easily swayed by the influence of others. But knowing who you are and what's important to you gives you the freedom to let other things go. Daniel knew that his relationship with God was what mattered to him, so it was easy to push away the rich food and wine at the king's table and to reject the power and wealth offered by the king, even when those actions were risky. If you know what matters to you, you will find it easier to walk away from things you value less. Daniel loved God more than he loved his own life. He was willing to face almost certain death in the lion's den. What are you willing to risk for the things you value? Is your relationship with God one of the things you value?

Apocalypse

The Book of Daniel is an example of apocalyptic literature. When we hear the word "apocalypse," we tend to think of a cataclysmic battle at the end of the world, but the apocalypse comes from a Greek word meaning "unveiling." Apocalyptic literature unveils a vision of the future, a vision in which good and evil are sorted out, with the evil punished and the good rewarded. Many of these writings come from periods of great turmoil and suffering. They were written to strengthen and encourage people who faced persecution because of their beliefs.

In addition to Daniel, the Book of Revelation and parts of the Book of Ezekiel are examples of apocalyptic literature. Since they are the same type of literature, it's not surprising that they share some similar characteristics. They rely heavily on dreams and visions filled with graphic and sometimes gruesome language. Symbols and numbers play important roles, often revealing hidden meanings. In some cases, it may be difficult for us to fully understand these symbols since their meaning may be obscured by time. These books tell of battles between good and evil but always make it clear that the outcome will be in accord with God's plan. Though the battle may be fierce and good people may suffer greatly, in the end, God will win, and the good people who held firm will be rewarded.

Because apocalyptic language speaks of an unseen future using symbolic language, the meaning of these texts is often difficult to grasp. Many people interpret these texts as foretelling a future that we might expect to see. Countless interpreters have used these texts to explain current events, aligning specific people with the forces of good and others with the forces of evil. In most cases, these interpretations tell us more about the interpreter than they do about the text. They remind us we should try to understand the biblical text, accepting the challenges it presents to the way we live rather than using the text to support our established views.

Different Names

One of the most confusing things about reading the Bible is that the same person or place often goes by more than one name. For example, when he was received into the royal household, Daniel was given a Babylonian name, Belteshazzar, in addition to his Hebrew birth name. Similarly, Esther was the Persian name given to the Jewish orphan Hadassah. In these cases, the different names show the clash of cultures that often existed in the region. The same thing often happens in our culture as people with names of a particular ethnicity "Americanize" their names when they come to the United States.

In other cases, God gives people a new name. Abram became Abraham (and his wife, Sarai, became Sarah) when God made his covenant with them. Jacob became Israel after he wrestled with an angel. Simon became Peter after he affirmed his belief that Jesus was the Messiah. In these cases, the name change reflects a deeper change in the individual's identity—and in his or her relationship with God.

Some biblical places go by more than one name. Mount Horeb is the same place as Mount Sinai. The Sea of Galilee, the Sea of Tiberius, and the Lake of Genessaret are three names for the same body of water. Many different nations lived in this region over the centuries, and they gave these places different names. Cities and even countries still change names. The country that used to be Rhodesia is now Zimbabwe, and Zaire became the Democratic Republic of the Congo. The city that was Constantinople is now called Istanbul. New Amsterdam became New York. Sometimes, the name of a country depends on where you live. The group of islands near Antarctica is called the Falklands if you live in Britain and the Malvinas if you live in Argentina.

The Bible was compiled over hundreds of years and tells the story of God's love for his people over more than a millennium. The events recounted in the Bible happened in a place of great turmoil during those years. It's not surprising that not everything stayed the same. Don't let the changing names confuse you.

Read More About Daniel

The Book of Daniel

Questions to Think About

1. What people, places, or things tend to draw you away from the Lord's path?

2. What things help to strengthen your resolve to obey God?

3. What one thing can you do today to help you resist the temptations you face?

Prayer

God,
I want to follow you,
but sometimes it's hard.
It just seems easier to follow the crowd.
Please fill me with your strength
so I will do what is right.
Amen.

Chapter 13

Liam: A Real-Life John the Baptist

He must increase; I must decrease.

JOHN 3:30

Liam and Seamus weren't just brothers; they were friends. Even though they were very different, they respected each other's skills and got along well. Seamus was always the center of attention, but that didn't seem to bother Liam. In fact, Liam went out of his way to tell other people about Seamus' accomplishments. He always seemed so proud of his kid brother.

But Liam did more than talk. He went out of his way to make things easier for Seamus. Liam took on extra chores at home so Seamus would be able to continue serving as a volunteer at the homeless shelter and be on the student council. When Seamus made the swim team, Liam woke up early twice a week to drive him to morning practice. It seemed as though Liam was always on the lookout for things he could do to make Seamus' life easier.

Seamus didn't take Liam's efforts for granted. He knew he'd never be able to do everything he did if it weren't for Liam. Seamus appreciated everything Liam did for him, and he tried to reciprocate whenever he could. Even more, Seamus told anyone who asked that Liam was the best guy he knew.

Even though Seamus got more attention from people, Seamus and Liam knew they were a team and that they were stronger together than they were on their own.

Who Is John the Baptist?

Before we meet John the Baptist, we meet his parents, Zechariah and Elizabeth. Zechariah was a priest, and both he and Elizabeth were good and holy people. However, they had no children. Given that they were both older, it seemed they would never have a child. Then one day, while Zechariah was serving in the Temple, the angel Gabriel appeared and told him that he and Elizabeth would have a son. Gabriel told him his son, to be named John, would be set apart to serve God, even from birth. Zechariah had trouble understanding all of this. Seeing an angel? Having a son at his age? When he expressed his doubt to Gabriel, Gabriel told him that, as a sign of the truth of these words, Zechariah would be unable to speak until the child was born.

Fast-forward nine months, and the elderly Elizabeth delivers a son! The neighbors were already talking about Zechariah's inability to speak, and now this! When Elizabeth said she would name him John, the neighbors suggested that she name him after his father instead, asking Zechariah to confirm their suggestion. Zechariah called for a writing tablet and wrote that his son should be called John. With that statement, Zechariah was able to speak again. His first words sang the praises of God who had blessed him with the gift of a son.

We know nothing of John the Baptist's upbringing. The next time we see him, he's living in the desert, attired in simple clothing and eating whatever he can find. John preached to anyone who would listen, calling on them to acknowledge their sins, repent, and begin to live holier, more righteous lives. He reminded people that being born an Israelite was not enough. People had to live their faith. People should share their belongings with those in need and be satisfied with what they had. They should be honest. Those who acknowledged their sins could be baptized in the Jordan River, the washing a symbol of their desire to start anew.

John told the people time and again that he was not the Messiah. Instead, his role was to prepare the way. John was clear that the one to come would be far greater than he was. One day, while John was preaching and baptizing, Jesus approached him, requesting baptism. (Jesus was related to John in some way; their mothers were relatives.) John seems to have recognized Jesus and was taken aback by this request, since Jesus had no sins to acknowledge. Jesus insisted that John comply with his request. After Jesus had been baptized, the heavens opened, and the Spirit came down in the form of a dove and rested on him. Jesus had great respect for John. He once told his followers that John was the greatest man ever born!

John continued preaching after Jesus' baptism. Unfortunately, John's preaching seems to have angered King Herod and his wife. Herod had married Herodias, his brother's former wife, a union forbidden in the religious law. John called them to account for this behavior. Telling a king he is wrong can be dangerous—a fact that John the Baptist learned the hard way. Angered by John's preaching, Herod threw him in jail, but John was kept in jail (rather than going to trial or being executed) because, while the preaching made him angry, Herod liked listening to him.

Herodias' feelings weren't quite so conflicted. She hated John. When her daughter performed a dance for Herod's dinner guests, Herod invited her to name her reward, no matter how outlandish. (He offered her up to half of his kingdom!) At Herodias' urging, the daughter asked for the head of John the Baptist. Trapped by his impulsive promise, Herod had John executed, and Herodias was given her reward. John's followers claimed his body and made sure his body received a proper burial.

What Can John the Baptist Teach Us?

John the Baptist lived his life on the fringes of society, but he can teach us a lot. First, John spoke the truth, no matter what. He called people to change their lives, living justly and caring for those in need. Even though he didn't set out to hurt people, he clearly ruffled feathers. Many people respond to being challenged to improve by attacking the messenger. John shows us we need to remain committed to speaking and living the truth even when it isn't popular.

Second, John the Baptist reminds us that God has set each of us apart for a special task. Each of us is important to God. We have a contribution to make to building the kingdom of God and sharing the good news. Through our words and actions, each one of us is called to help prepare the way for Jesus. John the Baptist shows us that we should not focus on promoting ourselves, but on letting Christ shine through us. Our selfish desires should always take a back seat to doing what God calls us to do. We must learn to live by God's will, not ours.

Nazirites

John the Baptist was a Nazirite, as were Samuel, the judge and prophet; and Samson, the great hero of Israel. A Nazirite was a person who made a vow to dedicate himself or herself to God for a specific period of time, sometimes for life. Nazirites were seen as set apart for God's service. They did not cut their hair, drink wine or consume anything made from grapes, and could not come in contact with any dead bodies. The births of both Samson and John the Baptist were foretold by angels. These angels directed the parents to raise their sons as Nazirites from birth, assuring that they would be dedicated to God from the very beginning. (The angel even warned Samson's mother not to drink wine while she was pregnant, so as to maintain his Nazirite status "from the womb.") Samuel's mother, Hannah, offered to raise her son as a Nazirite as a way of thanking God for the gift of a child.

Nazirites did not have specific tasks to perform; they were simply dedicated to God and to whatever task to which he called them. God called the three Nazirites we meet in the Bible to very different tasks. Samson was a warrior who helped to protect Israel. Samuel was a prophet. John the Baptist was the herald of the Messiah. Though their tasks were different, they had one thing in common: They responded to the Lord's call.

Two Kinds of Baptism

Was the baptism of John the same as the baptism we received? No, it was not. John the Baptist baptized people in the Jordan River for the forgiveness of sins. For the person baptized, John's baptism symbolized repentance and a desire to reform his or her life. That's why John was surprised that Jesus came to him to be baptized. Jesus didn't need to repent or reform.

Though Christian baptism does forgive sins (both original sin and personal sins), it also changes the person being baptized, incorporating him or her into the body of Christ. Christian baptism baptizes us into the death and resurrection of Jesus (see Romans 6:3–11). Obviously, that baptism could not exist before Jesus died and rose from the dead, so it is fundamentally different from the baptism of John. The grace of baptism calls and strengthens us to live our new life in Christ.

Read More About John the Baptist

Matthew 3; 11:2–19; 14:3–12
Mark 1:2–11; 6:17–29
Luke 1:5–25, 57–80; 3:1–22; 7:18–35
John 1:19–34; 3:22–30

Questions to Think About

1. What do you need to sacrifice to be a better follower of Jesus?

2. What distracts you from the tasks to which God has called you?

3. How do you allow Christ to shine through you?

Prayer

Lord,
as John the Baptist prepared the way for you,
may I bring you and your message
to the people I meet.
Help me to put you first
so that I point people toward you.
Amen.

Chapter 14

Henry: A Real-Life Mary

Mary said, "Behold, I am the handmaid of the Lord.
May it be done to me according to your word."

LUKE 1:38

Henry loved God. Really, he did. But sometimes it just seemed so hard to be a good follower of Jesus. It wasn't the little things like getting up for Mass on Sundays. And even though going to confession made him nervous, he always felt so much better afterward that it was worth it. And it certainly wasn't religion class or youth ministry. Henry liked learning and talking about his faith.

No, the hard part was trusting in God's plan and saying yes to God's will. Henry knew God would never ask anything of him that he couldn't do, but sometimes it seemed God was overly optimistic. Every time Henry made a decision, he tried to think about what God would want him to do. Sometimes, that meant saying no to things Henry wanted to do—like party with his friends. Other times, it meant doing things he'd rather not do, like giving up his free time to help out at the homeless shelter or not buying things he wanted so he could give more to charity. Saying yes to God all the time was hard, but Henry kept trying.

Who Is Mary?

Scripture doesn't tell us anything about Mary's life as a child. When we first meet her in the Gospel of Luke, she is living in Nazareth, betrothed to Joseph, a man who was a distant descendant of King David. One day, Mary was visited by the angel Gabriel, who informed her of God's plan for her. God wanted her to be the Mother of the Son he was sending into the world to redeem humanity. Mary had to have been frightened by this request. When she was discovered to be pregnant, Joseph would know the child was not his. He could reject her. Then she and her child would have nowhere to go. Saying "yes" to the angel's request meant risking her security and her plans for the future. But Mary trusted in God and said "yes."

The angel also told her that her relative Elizabeth was expecting a child as well. Elizabeth was an older woman, thought to be well past the age when she could have a child. Despite her own pregnancy, Mary immediately traveled to Elizabeth's home to help her. When Mary arrived, Elizabeth's child (whom we know as John the Baptist) leapt in her womb, as though he recognized Mary and her Child. Elizabeth, too, recognized that Mary was carrying the Savior of the world. Mary responded to Elizabeth's greeting with a beautiful hymn praising God. This hymn, called the *Magnificat* from its first word in Latin, is based on the hymn sung by Hannah, Samuel's mother (see 1 Samuel 2). It recognizes the blessings given by God and praises God for remembering those people who are all too often forgotten by the world.

Mary and Joseph traveled to Bethlehem to comply with a Roman census. Imagine traveling, mostly on foot, in the very late stages of a pregnancy! While in Bethlehem, Mary gave birth to her Son in a stable, because there was no other place available to house her and Joseph. She had no friends or relatives to assist her. The first visitors were strangers, shepherds drawn in from the field, probably still smelling like sheep.

The Gospel of Matthew tells us that later visitors were more prestigious, Magi from the East. (Magi were usually from priestly families and had some sort of special knowledge. These Magi read signs in the stars.) These Magi brought rich gifts, but they also brought danger, because they had warned King Herod that a new king had been born. Threatened by the prospect of a new king, even one who was still a child, Herod had all the boys in Bethlehem under the age of two murdered. Jesus survived this massacre because an angel had warned Joseph in advance. Joseph took Mary and Jesus to Egypt where Herod would have no authority. Mary must have been terrified by the prospect of losing her child and stressed by another long journey—this time with a newborn in tow. Ultimately, after Herod's death, Mary, Joseph, and Jesus were able to begin their family life in Nazareth.

That doesn't mean that Mary's sorrows ended there. The Gospels recount only one incident from Jesus' childhood. When Jesus was twelve, the Holy Family went to Jerusalem for Passover. Jesus stayed behind in the Temple, frightening Mary and Joseph, who had no idea where he was.

Mary makes her next appearance early in Jesus' ministry. She, along with Jesus and his disciples, attended a wedding in Cana. When the newly married couple ran out of wine, Mary asked her Son to help them, resulting in Jesus' first miracle: turning water into wine.

Mary is in the background throughout Jesus' ministry. She may be considered Jesus' first and best disciple. She heard and kept God's word (see Luke 11:27–28). She did the will of God (see Mark 3:35), saying "yes" to the angel's request. She even followed her Son to the cross and stood at its foot with Mary Magdalene and the disciple Jesus loved (see John 19:25–27). When Jesus saw her standing there, watching her only child die a horrible death, he gave her into the care of his disciple, ensuring that she would be taken care of as long as she lived.

Mary appears one final time in the Bible. After Jesus' resurrection and ascension into heaven, Mary joined the apostles and some other disciples in Jerusalem, praying and waiting for the promised gift of the Holy Spirit. The same Spirit who came upon her when she conceived the Son of God would come over the gathered believers and bring the Church to birth.

What Can Mary Teach Us?

The first thing Mary teaches us is the importance of saying "yes" to God. We can never be our best selves or truly happy if we do not follow God's plan for us. The Bible shows us that this assent to God's will doesn't mean our lives will be easy or free of problems. Mary's life was difficult, filled with hardship and sorrow. But she accepted the difficulties that came her way, trusting that God would take care of her. Mary trusted that God would be with her, guiding, supporting, and empowering her to do his will. Because of her trust, God made her the vessel of our salvation. If we, like Mary, embrace God's will, we can live forever with her and her Son, Jesus, in heaven.

Throughout her life, Mary showed concern for those in need. Whether it was her relative, Elizabeth, or the newlyweds at Cana, Mary paid attention to what people needed and did what she could to help them. Often, we are more than willing to help those who are in need. The problem is that we are not attentive to those needs. Paying attention to others, especially those who are forgotten, requires a committed effort to look for ways to help. If we're constantly focused on our own needs and wants, it's easy to remain unaware of what others need.

Mary models trust for us in two other ways that seem to go against what our society teaches. First, she allows herself to be given to Jesus' beloved disciple. Later, she lives in the care of the community of disciples waiting for the Holy Spirit. Our culture prizes independence and relying on oneself. Sometimes, those who need and accept help are ridiculed. Mary reminds us that everyone needs the help of others. Even though our relationship with God is the most personal relationship of our lives, our faith is not just about "me and Jesus." Our relationship with Jesus brings us into relationship with his body, the Church. Together, we care for one another, build up one another's faith, and bring the Holy Spirit to the world.

Mother of God

The Bible tells us that Mary was the Mother of Jesus. We understand that human beings have mothers. It's much harder to understand that Mary was also the Mother of God. How can God, who existed before all things, have a mother? Whether Mary could be called the Mother of God was an important debate in the early Church.

Still, for more than 1,500 years, the Church has affirmed that Mary is the Mother of God. But what does that mean? In truth, it says less about what we believe about Mary than what we believe about Jesus. If we truly believe that Jesus was both God and human, two natures in one person, Mary has to be the Mother of that whole person, making her both the Mother of Jesus *and* the Mother of God.

Model of Prayer and Discipleship

We typically refer to Mary as Mother—Mother of God, Mother of the Church, even the Blessed Mother. But as important as her motherhood is, she is even more. Mary is a model for us in prayer and discipleship.

Several times, the Gospel of Luke says Mary reflected in her heart on what was happening. This reflection is an important part of prayer and a habit we should try to develop. Following Mary's example, we should take time each day to pray and reflect on what has occurred, looking for how God was present in our day and how we responded to his invitation to follow him.

This reflection will help you emulate Mary's example of discipleship and accept God's will in your daily life. God invites us to follow him each day, and like Mary, we should try to affirm his will for us. When we spend time reflecting on the ways God is present and working in and through us, we get better at seeing his invitations when they occur. Then we can try to follow Mary's example and be a model and spiritual mother to others.

Read More About Mary

> Matthew 1:16, 18–25; 2:1–23
> Mark 3:31–35
> Luke 1:26–56; 2:1–52; 11:27–29
> John 2:1–12; 19:25–27
> Acts 1:13–14

Questions to Think About

1. When has God invited me to follow him? How did I respond?

2. What can I do to be more attentive to the needs of those around me?

3. How do I allow myself to both care for others and be cared for by them?

Prayer

> *Jesus,*
> *help me to be like your Mother,*
> *saying "yes" to God's will,*
> *helping those in need,*
> *and staying close to you all my life.*
> *Amen.*

Chapter 15

Joanie: A Real-Life Andrew

He first found his own brother Simon and told him,
"We have found the Messiah."

JOHN 1:41

Joanie wasn't just friendly. She was great at making people feel welcome and at home. She was always the person asked to show new students around the school. She loved serving as a greeter at her church. At youth-ministry events, without being asked, she'd make sure that everyone was involved in the activities. She had a knack for knowing how to get people involved. The best thing about Joanie is that she recognized other people's gifts without being jealous of them. She was able to invite them to share their gifts for everyone's benefit.

Though Joanie was good about inviting people to share their gifts, she also shared her greatest gift: her faith in Jesus Christ. She wasn't the sort of person who insisted on giving her testimony to everyone she met. She just lived her faith out loud. She talked about going to Mass and confession the way other people talked about going to the mall. She didn't hesitate to mention something she'd read in the Bible when talking with her friends. When she decided to do (or not do) something, she'd explain the faith principles underlying her decision.

Joanie's love for Jesus made her happy. Her happiness and love for God showed in everything she did. People were drawn to her because her joy made her fun to be around. If someone asked her what made her so happy, Joanie invited them to church. Maybe they, too, could meet the Lord she loved.

Who Is Andrew?

Andrew was the brother of Simon Peter (we don't know which one was older). The two brothers worked together as fishermen and were among Jesus' first followers. Andrew was one of the twelve apostles selected by Jesus and commissioned to go out and preach the good news. Though Andrew was Peter's brother, he was not one of the three apostles (Peter, James, and John) singled out by Jesus as witnesses to the raising of Jairus' daughter (Mark 5:35–43), the transfiguration (Matthew 17:1–8), and the agony in the Garden of Gethsemane (Matthew 26:36–46). There is no evidence that Andrew was jealous of the extra attention and authority Jesus granted to his brother.

According to the Gospel of John, Andrew was a disciple of John the Baptist. When John saw Jesus, he called him "the Lamb of God" (John 1:29) and encouraged his disciples to follow Jesus. Andrew went and listened to Jesus. Inspired by Jesus' message, Andrew went and got his brother Peter, introducing Peter to Jesus and encouraging him to follow Jesus. Andrew's bringing Peter to Jesus is part of a pattern of action in the Gospel of John. Andrew is mentioned by name two more times. In both cases, he is bringing people to Jesus.

Once, Jesus was preaching in an out-of-the-way place. He asked the disciples how they could get enough food for the people to eat. Most of the disciples were stymied by this question—buying food for so many people would cost a fortune! But Andrew brought a young boy to Jesus. The boy had five loaves and two fish. Andrew wasn't sure how such a small quantity of food would help with such a large crowd, but he brought forward what was available. You may know what happens next. Jesus took the loaves and the two fish, said the blessing, and distributed the food to the crowd. Not only did everyone get enough to eat, there were leftovers!

The final time Andrew is mentioned in the Gospel of John, Jesus is preaching near Jerusalem. Some Greeks had come to hear Jesus preach, and they wanted to meet him. They asked Philip, one of the other apostles, to introduce them to Jesus. Philip told Andrew about the request and, together, they told Jesus. So, once again, Andrew brought people to Jesus.

What Can Andrew Teach Us?

Andrew teaches us that every person who believes in Jesus is called not only to follow Jesus but to lead other people to Jesus as well. Helping people know and follow Jesus isn't just the job of priests, nuns, and missionaries. All the baptized are called to do their part. Every Christian is called to the ministry of evangelization.

Evangelizing doesn't mean you have to travel far from home to preach the Gospel to those who have never heard of Christ, or even start preaching publicly in the streets. (While not everyone is called to this task, some people are. Is this the work God is calling you to do?) You can be a missionary without leaving your school or your neighborhood. Evangelization simply means sharing the good news that, through his death and resurrection, Jesus opened the gates of heaven so we can live free from the consequences of sin and in the light and grace of God forever.

Many, if not most, of the people in our lives have heard the Gospel already. They may be baptized and have practiced their faith in the past, but now have no relationship with Christ and his Church. Their faith needs to be reinvigorated by having a new encounter with Jesus. This encounter will help them reestablish their relationship with Jesus and give new energy to their faith. This renewed encountering of Christ for people who have fallen away from the practice of their faith or for people who, though baptized, never really grew in faith is called "the New Evangelization."

So how can you be a missionary? How can you share the Good News—the Gospels, plus all the good news about Jesus—with everyone you meet? The first and most important thing you can do is to follow Jesus faithfully and with joy. The best way to share your faith is by living it, and you can't bring people to Christ if you aren't near him yourself. (You won't be perfect. That isn't the point. The point is to keep trying.) You witness to your faith when you make attending Sunday Mass your top priority, when you confidently pray in times of need and joy, and when you take concrete actions to care for those in need simply because they are children of God. If your faith doesn't bring you peace and joy, why would anyone want it? (And, for that matter, why would you want to share it with others?)

Second, you can learn more about your faith. If you are living your faith boldly and with joy, people will notice. They may ask you questions about what you believe and why you believe it. Knowing your faith well can help you answer their questions. There are many ways to learn about your faith. Most parishes offer faith formation classes for all groups. You can study the Bible and the *Catechism of the Catholic Church*. You can read Catholic books, listen to Catholic radio or podcasts, and attend lectures or classes offered by your parish or diocese. Don't worry if you don't have all the answers. If someone asks you a question you can't answer, you can always research it together. After all, growing in faith is a lifelong experience.

Disciples and Apostles

People often use the words "disciple" and "apostle" interchangeably, but the Bible applies these words to different groups of people.

A disciple is a person who learns from a master teacher. Jesus' disciples were the people who listened to him preach and followed him in his ministry. These disciples are never numbered or named. There is no way to know how many people heard Jesus preach over the course of his ministry and how many of those people began to follow him. We know that some people heard Jesus preach and walked away from him (see John 6:66), but others followed him to the cross (see Mark 15:40–41) and beyond (see Luke 23:50–56).

The apostles were a group of twelve disciples specifically chosen by Jesus and sent by him to preach the Gospel (see Matthew 10:1–15). They were Jesus' closest companions throughout his ministry on earth. There were twelve apostles, just as there were twelve tribes in Israel. When the number was reduced by the death of Judas, the apostles replaced him with Matthias (Acts 1:15–26). As other apostles died (all except John died as martyrs for the faith), they were not replaced, because they had remained faithful to their mission all their lives. Still, some other early leaders in the Church, notably Paul and Barnabas, were given the title "apostle" because they, too, were sent to preach the Gospel. Today, the Church understands the bishops as the successors of the apostles, called to preach the Gospel and build up Christ's Church.

The Apostolic Church

The apostolic Church is the name given to the Church in the years immediately after Pentecost. In these years, the apostles led the Church, preaching Christ crucified and risen for our salvation. They traveled throughout the known world to teach and preach, baptizing those who believed and building up the Church. The apostolic Church era ended with the death of the last apostle, likely toward the end of the first century after the birth of Jesus.

During this period, the Church was small, typically meeting in homes. It had no official status in the Roman Empire and, from time to time, was even persecuted by those in authority. Some Christians of this period (including almost all of the apostles) died for their faith, earning the title of martyr. Yet this period was a time of growth for the Church as it spread from Jerusalem throughout the Middle East, through Asia Minor (the area around modern-day Turkey) to Greece and even to Rome.

The apostles were not the only people who preached and taught in this era. Leaders like Ignatius of Antioch and Polycarp came forward in various communities. Their writings, though not inspired like the books of the Bible, were very influential in helping to build up the Church in its earliest years. We still read these texts today, not only to understand Church history, but also because they can teach us more about our faith.

Read More About Andrew

Matthew 4:18–10; 10:1–4

Mark 1:16–18

John 1:35–42; 6:1–15; 12:20–26

Questions to Think About

1. Why do you want to follow Jesus?

2. What obstacles stand in the way of your following Jesus more closely?

3. How do you share your faith with others?

Prayer

Jesus,
I want to follow you always.
Help me to be like Andrew
and share my faith with others,
leading them to you.
Amen.

Chapter 16

Becca: A Real-Life Bartimaeus

And many rebuked him, telling him to be silent. But he kept calling out all the more, "Son of David, have pity on me."

Mark 10:48

Becca was a church girl through and through. She loved Jesus and his Church, and she didn't care who knew it. She went to church every Sunday and sometimes on weekdays as well. If the youth ministry sponsored an activity, you could count on Becca being there.

Still, being a person of faith wasn't something Becca did. It was something she was. For her, following Jesus wasn't just about going to Mass and confession and participating in parish events. Her love for Jesus filled every part of her life. She prayed all the time—when she woke up, before she went to bed, before every meal, when she needed something, before she made a big decision, and when she wanted to say thanks. Praying and being with God was her way of showing God how much she loved him. In everything she did, Becca wanted to please him.

Becca never seemed embarrassed by her faith. Sometimes people snickered when they saw her praying or teased her about going to church or being too uptight and good. Sometimes these things stung a bit, but Becca knew what she wanted, and nothing would stand in her way. She was going to follow Jesus. It wouldn't always be easy, but it was worth it!

Who Is Bartimaeus?

Bartimaeus was blind. Because of this disability, he was unable to work, so he had to beg to survive. He sat by the side of the road leaving Jericho and begged for money from the travelers who passed by.

One day, Jesus and a large group of his followers were traveling along Bartimaeus' road. Bartimaeus must have heard of Jesus' reputation as a healer. When Bartimaeus heard that Jesus was passing by, Bartimaeus began calling out to Jesus, loudly begging him for help. Apparently, Bartimaeus raised quite a ruckus, because several people told him to be quiet. But Bartimaeus didn't listen to them. He kept calling out, making a commotion.

Finally, Jesus heard Bartimaeus and called to him. Bartimaeus tossed his cloak off and came to Jesus. When Jesus asked Bartimaeus what he wanted, without hesitation Bartimaeus asked that he be able to see. Jesus then healed Bartimaeus' blindness. Able to see, Bartimaeus followed Jesus and gave praise to God.

What Can Bartimaeus Teach Us?

For a man with such a small role in the Bible, Bartimaeus teaches us big lessons on the importance of prayer. First, he isn't afraid to ask God for what he needs. He shouts loudly, trying to attract Jesus' attention. When he's successful, he doesn't hold back from telling Jesus what he needs. He asks for sight, and his request is granted. Bartimaeus knew that trusting in God's love is never in vain. God wants us to have all that we need.

Second, Bartimaeus refused to be silenced. Even when people urged him to be quiet, he refused. While silence plays an important role in prayer—how can you hear God's voice if you're never quiet?—there are times when silence is the wrong choice. We should never be afraid to talk to God. God is always waiting to hear from us, even if it's been a long time. In the same way, we should not be silenced in our daily lives when speaking out can help someone in need. Being silent in the face of prejudice or bullying is easily seen as complicity or agreement. In such cases, even when people tell us to be quiet, we should follow Bartimaeus' example and continue to defend what is right.

Finally, Bartimaeus shows us that our top priority should be spending time with Jesus. When Jesus first called Bartimaeus over, Bartimaeus left his cloak behind. That cloak was likely Bartimaeus' only possession. It kept him warm in the cold and dry in the rain. He may have kept the money he collected from passersby in a fold of the cloak. By leaving the cloak behind, Bartimaeus abandoned all of his worldly goods to approach Jesus. Once Bartimaeus had regained his sight, his first action was to follow Jesus on his way. Finally, after years (perhaps a lifetime) of blindness, Bartimaeus didn't do anything to enjoy his new sight. He didn't go off to find a new job so that he could support himself without begging. He didn't seek out greater comfort and more security. He didn't even go back and get his cloak. He gave praise to God and began following Jesus.

Is prayer our top priority? What are we willing to walk away from so that we can talk with Jesus? All too often, we skip Mass in exchange for a few extra hours of sleep. We focus on owning the right clothes and best gadgets rather than living more simply so we can help those who lack the basic necessities of life. (No, a new gaming system is not a necessity.) Without taking time out to hear what God has to say to us, we won't know how to act when hard decisions or opportunities for holiness come our way. Even if we did, we wouldn't have the moral strength to follow through.

Following Jesus isn't easy. It means taking up Jesus' cross and accepting the suffering that comes with that decision. It means denying yourself things that will lead you away from Jesus—even if they make your life "easier" or more pleasant. It means judging every choice on whether or not it brings you closer to God. If you want to follow Jesus, you can learn from Bartimaeus' example.

Miracles

A miracle is an event that can't be explained apart from divine intervention. The key to understanding miracles is recognizing that God is the one acting. No matter who performs the miracle, God is the one in charge.

The Bible is full of miracles. The Gospels tell of Jesus healing many people, including Bartimaeus, Peter's mother-in-law, a paralytic, and lepers. Jesus freed people who were possessed by demons. He turned water into wine at the wedding of Cana, and he fed 5,000 with five loaves and two fish. He even raised Jairus' daughter and Lazarus from the dead.

But Jesus isn't the only person who performs miracles in the Bible. Elisha fed 100 people with twenty loaves. He also brought a widow's son back to life. Sent on mission by Jesus, the apostles reported miraculous healings. Even after Jesus' death and resurrection, miracles continued. Peter cured a crippled man who sat at the Temple gate. Peter raised Tabitha to life; Paul raised Eutychus.

Miracles continue even today. Before the Church canonizes saints, miracles are attributed to the individual's intercession. (People pray to a holy person who has died, asking that person to intercede with God to beg for divine intervention in a specific case. If the requested intervention occurs, that is considered proof that the holy person is in God's eternal presence—a saint.) Even though we live in a world that looks for scientific explanations for everything, miracles remind us that God continues to act in our lives.

Illness

The understanding of illness in the biblical world is very different from the way we understand illness today. Modern medical science has helped us to understand the causes of many diseases, to provide protection from them, and to offer treatments or cures. The people in the biblical world did not understand the causes of illness and disability. People believed that some illnesses were caused by demonic possession. They believed that other illnesses were punishments for sins—either that of the sick person or of his or her parents. These beliefs often led to those who were ill or disabled being isolated from the rest of society.

Though our understanding of illness has changed over the years, people with some illnesses, such as addictions and AIDS, are still shunned by many people. Some persons with physical or developmental disabilities are treated as second-class citizens and denied opportunities to learn, work, or even live in society. Many unborn children with genetic abnormalities are killed in their mother's wombs before they draw their first breath. Recent legislation allows people with serious illnesses to ask a doctor to help them end their own lives. Some countries even allow doctors to actively end their patients' lives (euthanasia).

Jesus, on the other hand, gave special attention to those who were ill. He gave them loving attention, healed them (even on the Sabbath, when such actions were forbidden in the law), and helped them reclaim their place in society. As Jesus' followers, we, too, must care for those who are ill, respecting their dignity until natural death.

Read More About Bartimaeus

Mark 10:46–52

Luke 18:35–43

(Bartimaeus is not identified by name in this passage.)

Matthew 20:29–34

(This passage seems to parallel Bartimaeus' story in Mark's Gospel, but this version refers to two men who are blind.)

Questions to Think About

1. What people or things keep you from following a prayer routine?

2. When are you tempted to remain silent when you know you should speak out?

3. What things can you do to follow Jesus more closely?

Prayer

Jesus,
I want to follow you.
I know it won't always be easy,
but I know you will be there to help me.
Let me be like Bartimaeus
and talk to you along the way.
Amen.

Chapter 17

Rosa: A Real-Life Mary Magdalene

Mary of Magdala went and announced to the disciples,
"I have seen the Lord," and what he told her.

JOHN 20:18

Rosa hadn't had an easy life. As her guidance counselor put it, she'd had issues. She never talked about them, even with her friends, but everyone knew she'd had a difficult past. By the time she got to high school, Rosa was working hard at putting her past behind her. She was working with a tutor so that she'd get caught up in school, and the guidance counselor was helping her get the rest of her life on track.

Rosa was really excited when she started to get involved in school and church activities. Maybe the tech squad and the youth ministry hospitality committee weren't the coolest groups to belong to, but for the first time in her life, Rosa felt like she was part of something. She was the most dependable person in both groups. You could always count on her to stick around until all the work was done.

Rosa was stunned when she walked by the principal in the hall one day, and she called to her by name. Mrs. Vickers thanked her for all she contributed to the school and invited her to become a school ambassador, visiting grade schools to talk to prospective students. Then Fr. Guttiérrez invited her to be on the spring retreat planning committee. Finally, Rosa had a place where she belonged. She couldn't wait to tell other struggling kids how good their lives could be.

Who Is Mary Magdalene?

We really don't know much about Mary Magdalene. The Gospel of Luke reports that seven demons had gone out from her, so we know that she experienced healing. After that, she seems to have followed Jesus as he traveled around the region, preaching to those who would listen. Along with other women like Joanna and Susanna, Mary Magdalene provided resources to support Jesus and the apostles as they traveled.

The next time we see Mary Magdalene, she is at the foot of Jesus' cross. All four evangelists (Gospel writers) record that Mary Magdalene was present when Jesus died. She remained faithful to Jesus to the very end of his life, accompanying him through the pain and shame of death by crucifixion, watching as he drew his last breath and completed his ministry on earth. After Jesus' death, she watched as he was taken down from the cross and accompanied Joseph of Arimathea as he placed Jesus in his tomb. Jesus was buried shortly before sunset, which began the Sabbath observance. No work—even anointing a body for burial—was permitted on the Sabbath. Mary Magdalene must have been dismayed that she didn't have time to properly prepare Jesus' body for burial. The Gospel of Matthew reports that Mary Magdalene sat by the closed tomb, keeping vigil.

Just before dawn on Sunday morning (the Sabbath had ended at sunset on Saturday evening), Mary Magdalene, along with some other women, went to the tomb. They brought oils and perfumes, the substances typically used to anoint a body before burial. Since they hadn't had time to anoint Jesus before the Sabbath, they intended to do it now. As the women traveled to the tomb, they wondered if they would be able to reach the body. After all, the tomb had been sealed with a large stone, and the women weren't strong enough to move it.

Imagine Mary's surprise when she arrived at the tomb to see the stone already rolled back! The first fear had to be that Jesus' grave had been robbed (and the body stolen) during the night. But this fear was soon relieved. An angel appeared to Mary Magdalene and the other women and told them that Jesus had been raised from the dead. He was no longer dead, but living once again. The angel charged the women to carry the message of Jesus' resurrection to the apostles.

The Gospel of John recounts a meeting between Mary Magdalene and the risen Jesus. Mary is sitting in the garden, still weeping. She sees a man she assumes is the gardener. This man calls her by name, and she recognizes that he is Jesus, risen and glorified (which explains why she didn't recognize him at first). Jesus tells her not to cling to him but to carry the good news to the eleven apostles (Judas was already dead): Jesus was risen, and death was defeated.

What Can Mary Magdalene Teach Us?

Even though the Gospels speak about Mary Magdalene only a few times, she can teach us a lot. First, she reminds us that righteousness, or righteous living, doesn't mean always being perfect. No matter what sins we have in the past or weaknesses we have in the present, they are not our whole story. No matter where we are from, what we have done, or what has happened to us, Jesus is always waiting to offer us healing, comfort, and a home (see also the story of King David earlier in this book).

Also, she reminds us that righteousness comes from remaining close to Jesus. Jesus called Mary by name. He knew her, and she knew him. In the same way, we need to spend time in prayer, getting to know Jesus, so when he appears and calls our name, we recognize him and respond. Knowing and loving Jesus, Mary Magdalene realized she couldn't go back to her old life but needed to learn to imitate Jesus' words and actions, the purest definition and example of what is right and good.

Once Mary Magdalene became a disciple, she strived to remain faithful to Jesus, even in the face of suffering. Can you imagine how hard it must have been for Mary to stand at the foot of the cross, watching Jesus die? Righteousness means doing the right thing even if you don't want to, like helping at the homeless shelter instead of going to the amusement park with friends, or making a donation to the church instead of saving for a pair of expensive jeans. Being Jesus' disciple means denying yourself and purging yourself of selfishness so that you live in accord with God's will. While these things may seem tough now, you will know you are following Jesus faithfully and staying close to him.

Finally, Jesus charges Mary Magdalene with spreading the Gospel. By our baptism, each of us has the same charge. We are called to share the good news: that by his death and resurrection, Jesus has saved us from the powers of death and opened heaven for us so that we can live with God forever. Sharing the Gospel doesn't mean that we have to stand on street corners shouting at people to accept Jesus or go door to door handing out Scripture pamphlets. A righteous life that demonstrates Gospel values is the best preaching we can ever do. To be righteous, we need to realize that life on earth is not all there is. We really belong in heaven, so we have to judge our lives by heaven's standards. Having nice clothes and a fancy car don't matter in heaven. The things that matter in heaven include loving every person as a child of God, caring for those who are most vulnerable, and striving to know and live by the truth as taught by Jesus and his Church.

Who's the Real Mary Magdalene?

The fact that the Gospels don't say much about Mary doesn't mean that people have to fill in the blanks. Over the centuries, people have theorized about who Mary Magdalene really was and what role she played in Jesus' ministry. Some have theorized she was a former prostitute who, after meeting Jesus, spent the rest of her life doing penance for her sins. Others suggest she was some kind of super-apostle, perhaps earning that position because she was Jesus' wife. There is no evidence in sacred Scripture that either of these theories is accurate. For the most part, these theories were developed by reading things into the biblical text rather than by reading what the text actually says.

Don't let yourself be distracted by wild theories. Focus on what we know about Mary Magdalene. She experienced healing and, as a result, traveled with Jesus as he preached, helping to support his ministry. She remained a faithful disciple, following Jesus to the cross and even to the tomb. After Jesus' resurrection, she carried the news to the apostles, earning her the title of the "Apostle to the Apostles."

Stewardship

The Gospel of Luke tells us that Mary Magdalene, Joanna, and Susanna used their money to support Jesus and his disciples in their ministry. The apostles had abandoned their careers to follow Jesus (several were fishermen, and Matthew was a tax collector), so there was no other money coming in to provide food, shelter, and other necessities.

We are called to follow the example of these holy women by providing for the needs of the Church by sharing our time, treasure, and talent. This sharing of our gifts is called stewardship. Stewardship is founded in the realization that everything we have is a gift from God. Thus, we should respond with gratitude and give our gifts back to God. What we are able to give may be different at different times in our lives. Right now, you may not have much money to put in the collection basket, but you can share your time and your skills, volunteering to help out with the tasks that need to be done. At other points in your life, you may be able to donate more money, but you will have less time.

What you give and how much are not what really matters. The most important thing is that you give your best to God and help support his Church.

Read More About Mary Magdalene

Matthew 27:56–60; 28:1–10
Mark 15:40; 16:1–8
Luke 8:1–3; 23:50–56; 24:1–12
John 19:25; 20:1–8

Questions to Think About

1. What difficulties have you embraced to be a more faithful disciple?

2. How do you work to build your relationship with Jesus who calls you by name?

3. What do you do to help share the Good News (the Gospels and all the good news about Jesus) with people you meet?

Prayer

Lord,
thank you for calling me to a life of righteousness.
I know I haven't always been perfect.
Please help me to stay close to you
and to share my faith with others.
Amen.

Chapter 18

Charlie: A Real-Life Timothy

I entrust this charge to you, Timothy, my child, in accordance with the prophetic words once spoken about you.

1 TIMOTHY 1:18

Everyone agreed: Charlie was a great guy. He wasn't the best student or a star athlete, but he was a loyal friend and lots of fun. When a few kids started to get homesick on the youth group mission trip, Charlie was the one who started the mud fight to make people laugh and forget to be sad and afraid.

Charlie had always taken his faith very seriously. His mom and dad taught him to pray when he was a little boy. As soon as he was old enough, he became an altar server. After his confirmation, he began serving as a lector. If there was a youth-ministry event, Charlie was sure to be involved—whether it was a softball game, movie night, helping at the soup kitchen, or Eucharistic adoration. No one was really surprised when the pastor asked Charlie to take the youth seat on the parish council.

No one except Charlie, that is. Charlie was worried. The parish council included all leaders in the parish community, including the school principal, the pastor, and the parish business manager. Why would those people listen to what a high school kid had to say? What could he add to their discussions? Would anyone take him seriously?

Who Is Timothy?

Charlie has a lot in common with Timothy. Timothy was one of the earliest members of the Church. He was the son of a Greek father and a Jewish mother. Both his mother, Eunice, and his grandmother, Lois, were Jewish converts to Christianity. Because of their influence and example, Timothy chose to become Christian as well, and he built on that good foundation. He continued to grow in the faith, learning more about Jesus and trying to live a holy life. His words and actions won the respect of the other Christians in his hometown.

We don't know much more about Timothy's early years as a Christian, but whatever he did gained him the respect of the other Christians in Lystra. Lystra was a town in the part of the Roman Empire known as Asia Minor. That region is part of the modern-day nation of Turkey.

When Paul and Silas were preaching the Gospel throughout Asia Minor, they visited Lystra and spoke to the Christians there. Paul and his companions would typically travel throughout the eastern portion of the empire, preaching the good news of Jesus to everyone they met, be they Gentiles or Jews. Paul would also spend time with any Christians who might live in the area, offering them encouragement, teaching them, and making sure that their faith was strong and true. When Paul came to Lystra to preach, the other Christians told Paul about Timothy and his faith, speaking highly of his faith and his passion for the Gospel of Jesus Christ. Impressed by this testimony, Paul invited Timothy to join his missionary effort.

Once again Timothy showed his willingness to follow where Jesus led. He left his family and his ordinary life to follow Paul as he preached the Gospel. Timothy accompanied Paul on two of his three great missionary journeys. Sometimes Timothy traveled with Paul as he went from town to town. Other times, Paul would send Timothy ahead to make preparations or leave him behind to serve the new Christians when Paul had to move on. Timothy would teach the people about Jesus, strengthen their faith, and make sure they weren't led astray. Timothy also helped identify leaders who would stay with the community when he had to leave.

Despite being very young when he joined Paul and began to preach the Gospel, Timothy became one of the great leaders of the early Church. He is counted among the first bishops. Two of Paul's epistles were addressed to Timothy, offering him advice about how best to lead the people he was called to shepherd.

What Can Timothy Teach Us?

Timothy is a great companion for young people, because he began his work in the Church while still a young man. More than that, he showed two qualities that all Christians, no matter what their age, should try to develop in their own lives.

First, Timothy was open to learning from the people around him. In a Letter to Timothy, St. Paul described the "sincere faith that first lived in your grandmother Lois and in your mother Eunice and that I am confident lives also in you" (2 Timothy 1:5). Rather than rejecting what his elders had to teach him, Timothy kept an open mind and heart so he could learn from them.

Sometimes it may seem as though your parents, teachers, and priests don't really understand your life. It may seem as though there is nothing they can say that could help you. After all, when they were your age, life was different. Expectations and standards were different. Your friends might seem to be a better source of advice and guidance.

But Timothy would recommend a different path. He was willing to learn from those who had more experience with life and faith. He listened to their advice and was open to what they shared with him. He accepted Paul's leadership and followed his instructions. He was willing to learn from Paul even after Timothy had become the leader of the Church in Ephesus. Paul cautioned Timothy carefully about the need to always teach the truth and avoid being misled by false teachers. The need to learn and to seek the truth doesn't end when you graduate, turn twenty-one, or even become a parent. Openness to learning is a gift that keeps on giving throughout your entire life.

Second, Timothy demonstrates confidence in preaching. Timothy's love for Jesus was noticed by the people around him—so much so that they told Paul about him. When Paul gave Timothy the chance to preach the Gospel throughout the Roman Empire, Timothy leapt at the opportunity, even though he knew the work would be difficult and even dangerous. He gave his entire life to helping people learn more about Jesus and to live the way Jesus taught.

We, too, are called to preach and teach about Jesus through our words and actions. Though we may not face the dangers Timothy and Paul faced—imprisonment, shipwreck, and even execution—that doesn't mean our task is easy. Teaching about Jesus might mean choosing what is right instead of what is easy, even when it is unpopular or means we have to make sacrifices. People may laugh at us or accuse us of being strange or judgmental. Some days, it may seem like getting shipwrecked would be easier!

We must preach the Gospel of Jesus Christ through the choices we make. We can choose to be honest, to be giving, to treat other people as precious children of God. We can value people more than things. We can choose the lasting pleasure of growing closer to God over the temporary pleasure of feeling good. We can share our faith with our friends, telling them how our faith underlies the choices we make. We can invite others to learn with us, to pray with us, and to come to know Jesus in his Church with us.

In the end, we should choose to emulate Timothy in following Paul's advice: "Let no one have contempt for your youth, but set an example for those who believe, in speech, conduct, love, faith, and purity" (1 Timothy 4:12).

Jews and Greeks

Timothy was the son of a Jewish mother and a Greek father. To us, that doesn't sound like a big deal. While it's not unusual for families today to mix nationalities, cultures, and races, it was a much bigger deal in Timothy's day.

Centuries before the birth of Jesus, the Jewish people lost their independence as a nation. Instead, they lived under the control of more powerful empires. One of those empires belonged to the Greeks. But Greek influence in the Near East was not limited to the exercise of political and military power. It extended to culture, language, and philosophy as well. Many Jews spoke Hebrew, Aramaic, and Greek. Many Greeks showed great respect for the faith of the Jewish people, though not necessarily following the law in its entirety. These Greeks were called "God-fearers" to distinguish them from converts to the Jewish faith.

This religious difference was a major issue for the early Christian community. One of the big questions the apostles had to decide was whether Greeks (and other Gentiles—a word meaning all non-Jewish people) who wanted to become Christians had to embrace the entire Jewish law first. Ultimately, the apostles gathered in Jerusalem and decided that Gentiles did not need to follow all 613 commandments of Judaism. Instead, they needed only to avoid worship of other gods and immoral behavior. This decision helped Christianity spread throughout the Roman Empire—and ultimately, the world.

Mission and the Church

We use the word "mission" in lots of ways. We go on mission trips—often service projects to help people in need. We collect money for missions and support the work of people who go to all corners of the world to preach the good news that Jesus has risen from the dead and wants us to live with him forever.

But a "mission" isn't a two-week summer project or something that other people do. Instead, as Pope Francis reminded the young people at World Youth Day in Rio de Janiero in 2013, all Christians are called to be missionaries by virtue of their baptism. Every Christian, no matter how old or young, must have a missionary spirit. That doesn't mean that every Christian is called to move far from home to preach the Gospel in the most remote corners of the world (though that might be what God is calling you to do!). Most of us will be missionaries in our hometowns—in our schools and workplaces, maybe even in our families.

We need to preach the truth and share our faith in whatever ways we can. We are missionaries when we miss soccer practice to go to Mass and let our teammates know why worshiping God matters. (You could even invite your teammates to join you!) We are missionaries when we don't follow the crowd into immoral behavior, instead keeping to the values that the Church teaches. We are missionaries when we give of our time, talent, and treasure to help those in need because they are children of God, made in his image and likeness. Doing our part in the mission of the Church requires both words and actions—believing what the Church teaches and living what we believe.

Read More About Timothy

Acts 16:1–5

1 and 2 Timothy

Questions to Think About:

1. Whose faith examples have inspired me? What about their faith life do I want to emulate?

2. How can I find reliable guides to help shape my religious life?

3. What choices can I make to help other people learn more about Jesus?

Prayer:

Jesus,
even though it may be hard,
I want to preach in your name.
Help me to seek the truth,
learning from those around me.
Help me to make the choices
that will lead me—and others—to you.
Amen.

Chapter 19

A Real-Life Jesus

As the Father loves me, so I also love you. Remain in my love.

Look in the mirror. (Put down the book if you have to.) What do you see? What do others see when they look at you? As a Christian, your goal should be that others see Christ through you.

Jesus has gone back to his Father in heaven, but he is still with us. He sent his Holy Spirit to guide us, and he is really and truly present to us in the Eucharist, strengthening us so that we can live as his followers. Jesus left his Church as his body here on earth. As members of his body, each of us has a responsibility to bring Christ to each person we meet. We are the hands, feet, and heart of Christ in the world.

The last chapter of this book is the one you write with your life. We can't wait to read it!

Who Is Jesus?

Jesus is the only begotten Son of God, born of the Virgin Mary and raised by her and her husband, Joseph, in Nazareth. We know little of most of Jesus' life, but he seems to have been raised as a good Jewish boy, learning to read the Scriptures and visiting the Temple on important feasts.

When Jesus was about thirty years old, he began the ministry for which he had come into the world. He was baptized by John the Baptist, and the Spirit came down upon him. Then, Jesus went into the desert for forty days where he was tempted by the devil. The devil offered him comfort, power, and riches to abandon his task, to disobey his Father and destroy the unity they shared, but Jesus remained strong and resisted these temptations.

Coming out of the desert, Jesus began his ministry, preaching and teaching throughout the region. He became known for his ability to heal those who were ill, and he began to draw large crowds. From those who listened to his teaching, he chose twelve apostles to be his closest companions. He commissioned them to spread his teaching even further.

Jesus' teaching had several important themes. First, Jesus spoke of the importance of single-hearted reliance on God. This reliance is based on the knowledge that God will care for his children always. Trust in God is never in vain, because God can bring good, even from things that seem to be bad. Second, Jesus taught that we must not judge our lives by the world's standards (and we shouldn't judge other people at all!). While the world esteems wealth and power, Jesus' ministry reminds us that God raises up the poor and humble. Third, Jesus offered his abundant mercy to any sinner who repented. Finally, we should follow Jesus' example, laying down our own lives to help those in need. Jesus preached a great paradox: If we are willing to give up our lives, we will be rewarded with eternal life with God.

Jesus' preaching and the crowds he drew were quite frightening to the authorities at the time. Israel lived under occupation by the Roman Empire. Any hint of rebellion was stopped immediately—often with violence. The leaders were afraid that a major rebellion would encourage the Romans to destroy the nation completely (which is what happened in the year 70). Threatened by Jesus' popularity and his challenging teachings, a group of Jewish leaders turned Jesus over to the Roman governor, Pontius Pilate. Jesus was condemned to death as a revolutionary. Jesus was tortured and crucified (a horrible punishment typically reserved for the most dangerous criminals). His few possessions—his clothes—were divided by his executioners. He died, abandoned by most of his followers, and was buried in a borrowed tomb.

But that's not the end of the story! Three days after Jesus' death, some of his female followers came to his tomb to complete the traditional burial rites that had been interrupted by darkness and the arrival of the Sabbath day of rest. When the women arrived at the tomb, the stone blocking the tomb entrance had been rolled back, and Jesus' body was gone. Angels appeared to the women, telling them Jesus was alive. He had risen from the dead! He had defeated death so we can live with God forever in heaven.

Over the next forty days, Jesus appeared to his disciples, eating and drinking with them, helping them fully understand that he was the Messiah promised by Scripture. At the end of these forty days, he went with the apostles to a mountain outside of Jerusalem. While they were there, Jesus was taken from their sight, returning to his Father in heaven. Ten days later, Jesus sent his Holy Spirit on the disciples gathered in prayer, giving them the courage to proclaim the good news of Jesus' saving death and resurrection. That proclamation continues even today, because Jesus is with us, "yesterday, today, and forever" (Hebrews 13:8).

What Can Jesus Teach Us?

Jesus is the Master Teacher. He teaches us everything we need to know to be able to live with him, his Father, and the Holy Spirit forever. First, Jesus was perfectly united with his Father. In all cases, he accepted the Father's will, even when that will meant death on the cross. Because we are sinful—unlike Jesus, who was sinless—we do not always follow the Father's will. Still, Jesus reminds us that, in everything, we should strive to live in accord with God's will.

Just as Jesus faced temptation in the desert, we will be tempted to do what is easy instead of what is right, to be selfish instead of caring. But Jesus resisted the devil's temptations, and his love and presence, especially in the Eucharist, can help us resist temptation as well. When we do fail, Jesus offers us his merciful forgiveness and a fresh start in the sacrament of penance.

Finally, Jesus teaches us the importance of looking out for the least ones in society. In fact, in his parable about the end times (see Matthew 25:31–46), Jesus speaks of the great king who separates the good from the bad. The good people are the ones who, in caring for the poor and vulnerable, cared for Jesus himself. We are called to look upon persons in need as though they are Christ, caring for them with the same love and respect we would give to Jesus. It is easy to ignore the forgotten ones in society, but can you ignore Christ?

The Meaning of Baptism and Eucharist

The sacrament of baptism makes us part of the body of Christ, the Church. It calls us to do Christ's work in the world. Each person baptized in the name of the Father and of the Son and of the Holy Spirit has a role to play in helping build God's kingdom. Though these roles are different, they are all important.

We are strengthened to live out our baptismal call by our reception of the Eucharist. In the Eucharist, we receive Jesus' Body and Blood. Jesus comes to dwell within us, to strengthen us, and to fill us with the grace we need to follow him each day.

Though we can be baptized only once, we can receive the Eucharist each time we go to Mass (up to twice a day), as long as we have fasted for at least one hour and we are not aware of having committed a serious sin without first going to confession. We should attend Mass as often as possible, including every Sunday and holy day, so we can be inspired by the word of God proclaimed in Scripture, offer our lives to the Father along with the perfect sacrifice of his Son, Jesus, and receive the Eucharist so we can live like Jesus, in union with the Father.

What's in a Name?

We often call Jesus "Jesus Christ" or "Jesus the Christ," but what does that mean? The name Jesus comes from the Hebrew word meaning "God saves." Jesus' name tells us his mission. The Father sent Jesus to us to save us from the power of sin and death.

"Christ" is not Jesus' last name. In fact, it's not really a name at all; it's a title. "Christ" comes from the Greek word that means "anointed"; its Hebrew parallel is "Messiah." Jesus was anointed by God so he could carry out his saving mission.

Read More About Jesus

The Gospels (Matthew, Mark, Luke, and John)

Questions to Think About

1. Who has been Christ to me?

2. How have I been Christ for others?

3. What one thing can I do today to be more like Christ?

Prayer

Jesus,
I love you and I want to follow you.
Please fill me with your Spirit
and help me to be more like you.
Amen.

Conclusion

The Bible is filled with hundreds of companions who can walk with you on your journey of faith. If this book had been filled with stories of all of the possible companions, it wouldn't fit in your backpack!

This book was an introduction, an invitation for you to delve into the biblical text for yourself so you can discover new friends and companions along the way. But how should you do that?

If you don't have a Bible, get one. Make sure it's a Catholic Bible so you will have all the books. Until you get a Bible, you can read one online at usccb.org/bible/index.cfm.

Set aside quiet time (maybe half an hour to start) and choose a story to read. The Bible is filled with different types of literature: narrative, poetry, letters, law, etc. You may want to start with something from a narrative book, since it is more likely to include people you can relate to. For example, you could choose a passage from one of the Gospels or from the Acts of the Apostles.

Read the passage slowly. The goal isn't to see how much you can read, but to read with care and understanding. While you read, don't let the unusual language and settings distract you. While the events of the Bible took place long ago and far away, they still speak to us. As you read a story, concentrate on one character, asking yourself:

What gifts does this character have?

What challenges does this character face?

How does this character relate to God?

Does his or her relationship with God change over time?

What parts of my life are similar to/different from the life of this character?

What can this character teach me about my relationship with God?

At the end of your reading, thank God for the example of your Bible companion. Pray that God will grant you the gifts that helped this character build a strong relationship with God and his people. Think about one thing you can do to use these gifts in your everyday life.

Happy reading! Now, go live your real-life faith!

✠

Ablaze
Stories of Daring Teen Saints
ISBN: 9780764-820298
Spanish: 9780764-821769

Following Christ isn't always easy. You need faith, courage, patience, and love.

Colleen Swaim looks at eight young souls who became saints for the against-the-current, selfless heroism of their teen years. In addition to inspiring stories, *Ablaze* includes maps, recipes, prayers, journal prompts, Scripture references, and reflection questions to help readers apply the experiences of the saints to everyday life.

Features: Saint Dominic Savio, Saint Teresa of the Andes, Saint Kizito, Blessed Chiara Luce Badano, Saint Stanislaus Kostka, Saint Alphonsa of the Immaculate Conception, Blessed Pedro Calungsod, and Saint Maria Goretti.

Radiate
More Stories of Daring Teen Saints
ISBN: 9780764-821479

Whether you are young or merely a youth at heart, you will be inspired by the heroism of these teenage saints. Young male and female teen saints from various places in the world are in this text; a total of ten stories in all. This sequel to *Ablaze* by **Colleen Swaim** will continue to set your heart ablaze with vivid storytelling, saintly challenges, prayers, images, and more.

The saints in *Radiate* are Saint Marie-Bernarde Soubirous (Bernadette), Saint Rose of Viterbo, Saint Lucy, Blessed Laura Vicuña, Saint Agnes of Rome, Saint Luigi Gonzaga, Saint Peter Yu Tae-chol, Blessed Ceferino Namuncurá, Saint Louis Ibaraki and the Japanese Martyrs, and Saint Gabriel Possenti.